mentoring
new **special**
education
teachers

*To my mentors: Dr. Gene Watson, Dr. Thomas Stich,
and Dr. Elliott Lessen. Thank you for letting me take the
best of each of you. You always did have plenty to share.*

—MLD

*I dedicated this book to my dad, Dr. Harry Forgan, Jr.,
who has always been my mentor and hero.*

—JF

mentoring
new special
education
teachers

A GUIDE FOR MENTORS AND PROGRAM DEVELOPERS

MARY LOU DUFFY
JAMES FORGAN

CORWIN PRESS
A Sage Publications Company
Thousand Oaks, California

For information:

Corwin Press
A Sage Publications Company
2455 Teller Road
Thousand Oaks, California 91320
www.corwinpress.com

Sage Publications Ltd.
1 Oliver's Yard
55 City Road
London EC1Y 1SP
United Kingdom

Sage Publications India Pvt. Ltd.
B-42, Panchsheel Enclave
Post Box 4109
New Delhi 110 017 India

Printed in the United States of America

Library of Congress cataloging-in-Publication Data

Duffy, Mary Lou.
Mentoring new special education teachers: A guide for mentors and program developers/Mary Lou Duffy and James Forgan.
    p. cm.
Includes bibligraphical references and index.
ISBN 0-7619-3133-3 (cloth) — ISBN 0-7619-3134-1 (pbk.)
    1.   Special education teachers—In-service training. 2.   Mentoring in education.
I. Forgan, James W. II. Title.

LC3969.45.D84 2005
371.9—dc22   2004018165

This book is printed on acid-free paper.

04   05   06   10   9   8   7   6   5   4   3   2   1

Acquisitions Editor:	Kylee M. Liegl
Editorial Assistant:	Jamie L. Cuvier
Production Editor:	Diane S. Foster
Copy Editor:	Mark Newton, Publication Services, Inc.
Typesetter:	C&M Digitals (P) Ltd.
Proofreader:	Penelope Sippel
Indexer:	Michael Ferreira
Cover Designer:	Michael Dubowe

Contents

Introduction

Overview

*M*entoring New Special Education Teachers is designed to assist educators who are developing a mentoring program for new special education teachers, for individuals selected to mentor a new special education teacher, and for new special education teachers. The field of special education experiences a frequent attrition of teachers, thus teacher retention is a prominent topic discussed in professional literature and at conferences. According to the Council for Exceptional Children (2000a), within the first five years of teaching, 4 out of 10 teachers leave the field of special education. This figure is alarming considering an *Education Week* report (2002) indicated that 98% of school districts report shortages of special education teachers. Furthermore, the number of new special education teachers predicted for the near future is astounding as current teachers retire, move into other education positions, or leave special education. According to Boyer and Mainzer (2003), during the past ten years the growth in the number of students with disabilities has increased by 30% where as the growth in teaching positions grew by 11%. More students are entering special education than there are teachers to teach them.

The Council for Exceptional Children (2000a) predicts that by the year 2005, over 200,000 new special education teachers are needed throughout the United States. Presently, there are no indications that the demand for new special education teachers will subside anytime in the near future. McLeskey, Deutsch-Smith, Tyler, and Sanders (2002) report in their review of research on the shortage of special education teachers that the shortage exists across all regions of the United States, is chronic and long term, and will worsen over the next decade. The need for mentoring programs, as a form of special education teacher retention, is vividly clear.

School districts are reacting to the shortage of special education teachers by using various strategies such as adopting the "grow your own philosophy" of training paraeducators from within school districts. Other districts are recruiting teachers from distant geographic areas where there are higher than average numbers of special education teachers. Additionally, states and school districts are implementing mentoring programs as a retention activity. According to Feiman-Nemser (1996), the magnitude of mentoring programs has increased with over 30 states mandating mentoring support for beginning teachers. Resource B contains a list of states that mandate mentoring programs. State education agencies and local school districts recognize that it is cost efficient to support and retain existing teachers as compared to the recurring costs of recruiting and training new special education teachers. Whitaker (2000) recommends that mentoring is provided to all beginning special education teachers. Her recommendation is gaining momentum across the nation as research data supports the success of mentoring programs.

The effectiveness of special education mentoring programs is encouraging. According to Bridges to Success (2003), the Oregon special education recruitment and retention project, districts which implemented strong teacher support systems achieved a five-year teacher retention rate of 70% to 80%. In addition, the Council for Exceptional Children (2000b) suggests that special education teachers who have the support of a mentor teacher are more likely to remain in the profession. Mason and White (2001) corroborate these findings as reported in their results that 91% of new special education teachers surveyed in a national mentoring induction project reported they were satisfied with their mentoring experience.

Bey and Holmes (1990) describe three primary reasons for implementing mentoring programs:

1. To help beginning teachers cope with "dissatisfactions, disappointments, and difficulties" (p. 51) in the first year of teaching.

2. To combat high turnover and to reduce attrition.

3. To improve teacher performance.

Designing an effective mentoring program to address the issues of new special education teachers is not as simple as finding the most experienced special education teachers and pairing them with the new teachers. Mentoring programs should be flexible enough to accommodate the needs of participants and should not simply specify mentor and mentee roles.

School districts recognize that special education mentors support the mentee from their hire date, before students arrive for the first day of school, and throughout the first school year or longer. Without special education mentors, school districts risk high rates of teacher attrition and a never-ending cycle of hiring, training, and replacing special education teachers. Without a supportive mentor, the new special education teacher is also placed in a situation that can become frustrating and unfulfilling. Mentors, through their guidance, insight, and communication provide emotional and mental strength for the mentee. Having an effective mentor can make the difference between the mentee's first year of teaching being successful or exasperating. Mentoring can make the difference between the mentee returning to teach a second year or leaving special education all together. Reminisce to your first days of teaching. Who guided you through the ups and downs of organizing your classroom, preparing and meeting the students, and delivering effective instruction while managing behavior? If you are reading this book as a mentor, you understand how important effective mentoring is to the first-year special education teacher.

As a special education mentor, your role is not to mold the mentees to walk, talk, think, and teach like you, but to listen to their frustrations, rejoice in their triumphs, provide insight when they have questions, and just be there when the mentees need a shoulder to lean on. The mentoring process will benefit you as you learn about yourself, share your teaching philosophy and beliefs, and examine your teaching actions that have become automatic over time but now need to be explained so the mentee can learn how you think and operate. One reward of mentoring a new special education teacher is that you experience growth in the mentee and in yourself.

The activities in this book are designed to help individuals create and deliver effective mentoring programs for new special education teachers. The content has been field tested with experienced special education teachers serving as mentors to new special education teachers. Teachers have reported satisfaction with the activities and have shared vignettes of their experiences, which appear throughout the book. According to Lloyd, Wood, and Moreno (2000), a training program for special education mentors should consist of (a) the role of the mentor teacher; (b) tactics for working with adult peers; (c) ways to establish rapport and trust with the new teacher; and (d) strategies to provide both positive and constructive feedback. This book includes content that addresses these recommended components as well as timely additional information related to critical issues in mentoring new special education teachers as noted by Griffin, Winn, Otis-Wilborn, and Kilgore (2003). In their review of new teacher induction in special education, the following effective features of mentoring programs are described: frequent contact between mentor and mentee, pairing both mentors and mentees in special education, the nonevaluative role of the mentor, the mentor and mentee's understanding of the mentoring process, personal characteristics of the mentor, emotional support, and forms of support.

Moreover, Whitaker (2001) identified five factors related to the challenges many new special education teachers encounter their first year of teaching. These factors include (1) an inability to transfer learning from theory into practice; (2) a lack of preparation for many demands of teaching; (3) reluctance to ask questions or seek help; (4) the difficulty of the teaching assignment and the inadequate resources provided; and (5) unrealistic expectations and the associated loss of a sense of efficacy. This book provides the most current information that also takes in hand Whitaker's findings on the challenges facing special education teachers.

CHAPTER DESCRIPTIONS

The six chapters in this book address issues related to becoming a mentor, effective communication skills, adult learner characteristics, needs of new special education teachers, supports for new special education teachers, and elements of designing a mentoring program. Included in Resource A is a two-day workshop for training special education mentor teachers. Educators will also find figures, tables, and appendices throughout the book that provide specific activities and resources for mentors and protégés in a user-friendly format.

Chapter 1 contains special education–specific information related to the concerns of new special education teachers. The needs of new special education teachers are discussed in relation to their diverse backgrounds. For example, some new special education teachers will be recent college graduates, experienced special education teachers new to a disability area or grade level, or out-of-field teachers starting a second career. Numerous mentor-mentee activities are located in this chapter.

Supports for new special education teachers are discussed in Chapter 2. The uniqueness of special education is further identified by the inclusion of topics such as collaborating with general educators, making accommodations, Individualized Education Programs (IEPs), and instructional strategies. In addition, the Council for Exceptional Children knowledge and teaching skills are linked to resources for mentors.

Chapter 3 contains critical elements for designing effective special education mentoring programs. Principles from the Council for Exceptional Children Mentoring Induction project are discussed in relation to activities presented in the book, e-mentoring, action planning, evaluating progress, and fading support are additional topics discussed. A mentoring activities calendar is located in Chapter 3.

Chapter 4 describes the process of identifying, recruiting, and selecting special education mentors. Educators will find a description of the skills needed by mentors, personality traits of mentors, and the roles and responsibilities of mentors. Also discussed are the benefits of mentoring a new special education teacher. Most chapters conclude with Web sites for mentors and "What if" questions for mentors to consider.

Chapter 5 contains content related to effective communication skills. All relationships, including the mentor-mentee relationship, are built on effective communication. Nonverbal and verbal communication skills are discussed as well as teaming and problem solving skills. Activities for practicing communication skills are included in this chapter.

Skills needed by mentors in the area of adult learning theory are discussed in Chapter 6. There are specific needs of adult learners that differ from school-age learners. Motivation and validating experiences shape the mentee's behavior. The importance of matching personalities is discussed as the mentors explore their personality styles and determine whether they match their mentee's personality.

Throughout this book the recurring philosophy is that the mentor should assist, not assess, the mentee (Feiman-Nemser, 1996). The mentor and new special education teacher are building a relationship based on professionalism and trust that would be compromised by evaluative actions from the mentor. The content of this book will facilitate the development of this mentor-mentee relationship using current information accompanied with valuable activities and resources.

Acknowledgments

Grateful thanks to the students and colleagues who willingly shared their mentoring stories for our book:

Patricia Weber

Margaret Hearndon

Jacqueline Merritt

Nicki O'Neill

Sylvia Ostbye

Amy Holley

Lisa Heinz

Mandy Horton

Deborah Brown

Kathy Huie

Elliott Lessen

Cheryl Miranda

Debby Brown

Jennifer Thomas

Chris Stevens

Lorenzo Diaz

Corwin Press gratefully acknowledges the contributions of the following reviewers:

Joan Bacon
Associate Professor, Special
    Education
Augustana College
Sioux Falls, SD

Jo Bellanti
Director, Special Education
Shelby County Schools
Bartlett, TN

Margaret H. Blackwell, M.Ed.
Executive Director
Exceptional Education &
    Student Services
Chapel Hill-Carrboro City
    Schools
Chapel Hill, NC

C. Denise Buckingham
Principal
Shawswick Middle School
Bedford, IN

Colleen Klein-Ezell, Ph.D.
College of Education
Exceptional Education
University of Central Florida, Brevard
    Campus
Cocoa, FL

Cindy L. Grainger
Special Education Coordinator
San Carlos USD # 20
San Carlos, AZ

Deborah E. Bordelon, Ph.D.
Associate Professor and
    Assistant Chair
Xavier University
New Orleans, LA

Wanda Routier
Special Education Teacher
Sugar Bush Elementary School
New London, WI

About the Authors

Mary Lou Duffy is an associate professor of Exceptional Student Education at Florida Atlantic University. Her interest in mentoring stems from her work with preservice and inservice teachers in the local school districts in South Florida. She has had the opportunity to work with new teachers to help them learn practical ways to solve management and instructional problems. She is a participant in Florida's Comprehensive System of Personnel Development (CSPD) regional partnership, housed at Florida Atlantic University. She and Jim Forgan both have presented workshops and information sessions on mentoring and mentor training.

Her other interests in special education include transition services for students and young adults with disabilities from school to work. She teaches courses both online and in traditional format on transition. Her experience with online courses has helped her become comfortable teaching using distance technologies.

James W. Forgan, Ph.D., is an Associate Professor of Special Education at Florida Atlantic University where he teaches undergraduate and graduate courses. He is the principal investigator for the Southeast Regional Comprehensive System of Personnel Development Professional Partnership, and he is on a United States Department of Education grant to increase the number of master's level minority special education teachers. He was a teacher of students with learning disabilities and behavior disorders at the elementary and middle school levels for six years in the Miami-Dade County Public Schools. His professional interests are in the areas of mentoring, social skills instruction, and assessment. He may be reached by e-mail at jforgan@fau.edu.

REFERENCES

Bey, T. M., & Holmes, T. C. (1990). *Mentoring: Developing successful new teachers.* (Report No. SP032484). VA. (ERIC Document Reproduction Service No. ED322118)

Boyer, L., & Mainzer, R. W. (2003). Who's teaching students with disabilities? A profile of characteristics, licensure status, and feelings of preparedness. *Teaching Exceptional Children, 36*(6), 8–11.

Bridges to Success. (2003). *Supporting early career special educators.* Retrieved June 25, 2003, from Western Oregon University: Oregon Recruitment and Retention Project Web site: http://www.tr.wou.edu/rrp/mentext.htm

Council for Exceptional Children. (2000a). *Bright futures for exceptional learners: An action agenda to achieve quality conditions for teaching and learning.* Reston, VA: Author.

Council for Exceptional Children. (2000b). *What every special educator must know: The international standards for the preparation and certification of special education teachers.* Reston, VA: Author.

Feiman-Nesmer, S. (1996). *Teacher mentoring: A critical review.* (Report No. EDO-SP-95–2). Washington, DC: Office of Educational Research and Improvement. (ERIC Document Reproduction Service No. ED397060).

Griffin, C. C., Winn, J. A., Otis-Wilborn, A., & Kilgore, K. L. (2003). *New teacher induction in special education.* Retrieved August 6, 2003, from http://www.coe.ufl.edu/copsse/main.php?page=019

Lloyd, S. R., Wood, T. A., & Moreno, G. (2000). What's a mentor to do? *Teaching Exceptional Children, 33*(1), 38–42.

Mason, C., & White, M. (2001). The mentoring induction project: Supporting new teachers—hints for mentors and mentoring coordinators. *Teaching Exceptional Children, 34*(1), 80–81.

McLeskey, J., Deutsch Smith, D., Tyler, N., & Saunders, S. (2002). *The supply of and demand for special education teachers: A review of research regarding the nature of the chronic shortage of special education teachers.* Retrieved July 19, 2003, from http://www.coe.ufl.edu/copsse/main.php?page=016

Washington Partners, LLC. (2002). *Education report: Report of public policy issues in American education.* Retrieved September 2, 2003, from http://www.ncea.com/NCEALegislativeReportArchive2002.html

Whitaker, S. D. (2000). Mentoring beginning special education teachers and the relationship to attrition. *Exceptional Children, 66*(4), 546–566.

Whitaker, S. D. (2001). Supporting beginning special education teachers. *Focus on Exceptional Children, 34*(4), 1–18.

New Special Education Teachers

1

VIGNETTE

In November, a new special education teacher came to our school to take the position of one of our teachers going on maternity leave. Although she had one year of teaching experience as a regular education teacher, she had no experience in exceptional student education. Good teaching is good teaching, but strategies for teaching students with disabilities are critical, not to mention the maze of paperwork that is inherent in our job. The teaching is the easy part. It's the paperwork that makes special education teachers crazy!

We worked together to make sure that she was off on the right foot, and thanks to the teacher who had left, no IEP annual evaluations were looming in the immediate future. This "too-good-to-be-true" scenario lasted about six weeks, and then it happened. In mid-December, the district required that all third-grade IEPs must be reviewed in response to the Third Grade Retention law passed by the Legislature. Not only did the IEPs need to be reviewed, but also revised in the areas of "present level of performance" and "goals" to reflect the five elements of reading instruction deemed essential by research. All this had to be completed by January 31, a task most veteran special education teachers would find daunting.

Together, we spent many hours together learning these new directives, implementing them on our computerized IEP program, and meeting with parents concerning the revisions and their child's new IEP. As far as my protégé was concerned, it was "sink or swim" and "take the bull by the horns" time all rolled into one. She never complained, and by the second week in January, she was feeling like a "pro." With a lot of hard work and a few late afternoons, we completed our reviews on time and developed a professional rapport that will last far into the future

—Patricia Weber

WHO ARE NEW SPECIAL EDUCATION TEACHERS?

The mentor teacher and mentee in the vignette experienced the rewards of a close and supportive working relationship that, fortunately, will remain intact after the mentee's first year of teaching in special education is complete. Without the support from the special education mentor, the mentee would have been "left to the sharks" to navigate the enormous paperwork maze initiated by the state and local school district. One may be thinking, Is this vignette a realistic expectation for beginning special education teachers to hold?

WHERE THEY COME FROM

The term "new special education" teacher holds different meaning for these individuals who took various routes to arrive in their current teaching positions. New special education teachers are as diverse as the students they teach. Mentees in this group may be graduates of traditional teacher preparation programs, experienced special education teachers new to the district or disability area, teachers with an education degree in another field, participants in alternative certification programs, or individuals without any educational training.

Traditional Teacher Preparation Programs. Traditionally trained special education teachers have completed formal teacher preparation programs that are likely approved by their state departments of education. Most university teacher preparation programs prepare teachers for positions in a cross- or noncategorical service delivery model. For example, in one southeastern state special education teacher certification is called Exceptional Student Education and covers kindergarten through twelfth grade. This certification enables a special education teacher to teach all levels and types of students with disabilities except for the severe, deaf, and blind. In Illinois, when certified in special education, you are classified as a Learning and Behavior Specialist and are able to teach the high-incidence disabilities. Traditional teacher preparation programs require individuals to complete many hours of course credit in teaching reading, mathematics, and special education strategies, as well as complete a supervised teaching experience. Upon graduation, many of these teachers may feel ready to take charge of their own classroom and teach without the continual supervision of a cooperating teacher. Although this group of beginning special education teachers may have the knowledge about how to teach students with disabilities, they do not have the depth of experience needed to independently sustain them through the bumps and pitfalls of the first year. Nor are they savvy to the district or school procedures. One beginning special education teacher, as quoted in Whitaker (2000a) says, "For the most part in school all we learned is theory . . . Nothing prepares you for teaching until you start teaching" (p. 2).

These beginning teachers may lack confidence in their abilities and require emotional support from their mentors. Reassurance and active listening will help build the new teacher's confidence, and, like their students, the mentee will need frequent reinforcement at the beginning of the year with a gradual fading of support. One way to view the support of the mentor teacher is to use the analogy of a builder who is remodeling a tall building. The teacher sets up scaffolding around a building to use as his support while working on a particular area. As each area is complete and strong, the builder removes the scaffolding. The mentor teacher is similar to the scaffold support, providing strong support that is gradually removed as the mentee gains confidence and experience. An effective mentor will be a valuable resource for this group of mentees throughout the first year of teaching.

In addition to recent graduates of traditional teacher preparation programs, a unique group of special education teachers who can benefit from having a mentor are experienced special education teachers who are first-year teachers in a new school district. These teachers may have rich backgrounds of teaching students with disabilities and may feel competent with their teaching skills, designing and implementing instruction and working with paraeducators and parents. Despite their experience, these mentees will still need support. Mentors can provide emotional support to these teachers and assist with issues such as the school district's policies and procedures, paperwork, and orientation to the school building.

Although most mentees welcome support, it is realistic to expect that some will not. Mentors must be prepared that some experienced special education teacher mentees may feel insulted that they were assigned a mentor. Some veteran special education teachers may feel that learning paperwork and procedures is simplistic and easily completed on their own, whereas others may view accepting help as a sign of deficiency. Lisa, a mentor teacher, was asked to mentor a new faculty member who was a seasoned teacher new to the school district. She explained, "I tried many times to contact my mentee by e-mail and telephone. I even left messages with her fellow associates. Just when I was about to concede, I received an e-mail from her. She politely and diplomatically informed me of her prior teaching experience, thanked me for showing interest and concern, and let me know that she had everything under control." Lisa was disappointed about her mentee's lack of interest, and one variable she attributed to the lack of success in the relationship was that the seasoned teacher was assigned to work with Lisa rather than given the chance to request a mentor. Had the new teacher asked for a mentor, Lisa believes the relationship would have been successful. Fortunately for Lisa, she found and mentored another teacher who valued her contributions.

Some special education teachers may have taught students with mild disabilities (e.g., learning disabilities) and, because of choice or assignment, began teaching students with severe disabilities (e.g., autism). The state department of education often requires this group of professionals to complete college coursework or participate in school district–sponsored skill development workshops to be considered certified teachers. For example, one of this book's authors, Jim, is a certified teacher in the area of behavior disorders. One year when teaching elementary students, he was considered out-of-field or uncertified according to state guidelines because his assignment was to teach a class of students with learning disabilities. Jim was required to submit his transcripts to the state for a coursework review or complete several courses in the area of learning disabilities to be considered an in-field teacher. In Jim's case, he had already completed ample coursework on learning disabilities and was granted certification in specific learning disabilities. If he did not have a strong background in the area of learning disabilities, his mentor could have provided curriculum support. Because many state departments of education focus on streamlining teacher certification by offering test-only routes or alternative routes to special education teacher certification, scenarios such as Jim's are becoming less frequent, and the number of out-of-field teachers is decreasing.

Out-of-Field Teachers. Some certified teachers may not be certified in special education (e.g., a teacher certified in middle grades who begins teaching special education). This type of teacher should have a solid understanding of the school culture and classroom management techniques but does not have strategic knowledge to design lessons for students with severe disabilities. The same principle would hold true for an elementary general education teacher who decided to teach special education students with mild disabilities. He or she may benefit more from curriculum support in specific learning strategies or making accommodations rather than from support in classroom management strategies.

Alternate Certification Programs. Mentees who have completed or are currently enrolled in alternative certification programs have a range of experiences. These individuals are typically embarking on a second career so they may have professional knowledge in one or more subject areas and may have worked with individuals with disabilities in the community. The increased development and use of alternative certification programs is growing as a result of the No Child Left Behind Act (U.S. Department of Education, 2002) and the nationwide critical shortage of special education teachers (Council for Exceptional Children, 2001). For example, Florida school districts are allowed to design their own alternative certification programs to provide uncertified mentees with the skills needed to become teachers. Some of the school districts in Southeast Florida have partnered with Florida Atlantic University's (FAU) Department of Exceptional Student Education Comprehensive System of Personnel Development to offer a collaboratively designed teacher development program. This program was designed through the expertise of special education personnel of the school districts and FAU faculty in special education. Mentoring programs built upon university-school partnerships can help promote the widespread use of mentoring programs and promote school reform because mentees learn new pedagogies and professional norms from their mentors (Feiman-Nesmer, 1996).

The FAU teacher development program is year long, delivered in an alternate format that consists of 12 modules containing content such as assessing student performance, writing lesson plans and IEPs, designing instructional programs, and using technology. Several local school districts have adopted this as their special education alternative certification program. Each local school district pays the mentee's discounted university tuition, and the mentee's complete the program as a cohort. Special education–specific alternative certification programs, like the FAU program, which are built on a university and school district partnership, often contain the skills and knowledge uncertified teachers need to become competent.

Many times the school district's generic alternative certification program is required for all teachers to complete. A generic program may help most teachers and provide general information on relevant topics, but it may not have the specialized content needed to ensure the success of special education mentees. If the generic alternative certification program is the only one available, the mentee will require even more support from his or her mentor teacher to learn the necessary skills to become a competent special education teacher.

Some mentees may be employed as special education teachers as they complete the alternative certification program, whereas others may have completed the alternative certification program before securing a teaching position. The needs of these mentees will vary depending on the quality of their alternative certification program, their completion or progress point in the program, and their backgrounds. In many instances, mentees who have completed an alternative certification program require less support than those still participating in the program. Other mentees with strong content backgrounds, such as the case of a former engineer who is now teaching high school math to students with disabilities, will require less support in the content area and greater support in areas such as designing differentiated lesson plans, making accommodations, and classroom management. Mason and White (2001) caution that, "Teachers trained under alternative certification programs need more help and guidance than the typical mentoring program provides" (p. 80). Mentors and mentoring program developers will have to closely monitor the needed supports of this group.

Individuals Without Any Educational Training. The mentee with a degree in psychology who is teaching students in special education needs a high level of support in all areas, including teaching reading and math, learning strategies, managing behavior, as well as designing lesson plans and writing IEPs. Overall, this group of new special education teachers has minimal teaching skills, and they are employed in jobs for which they are not fully qualified. These mentees will remain in the survival mode the longest, often feeling that they are simply trying to make it through the school day. The same cautions of Mason and White (2001) apply to this group, as they will require the highest level of supports including emotional, instructional, and classroom. Given the diverse range of skills that the mentees without any educational training have, the mentor will need active listening skills to determine the most important areas to provide support.

First-year special education teachers without a background in education or knowledge of a specific content area will rely heavily upon the mentor's guidance to successfully complete their first year of teaching. Some mentees may not know where they need the most support, and, in this case, the mentor can use the checklist provided in Table 1.1 to pinpoint areas of low, moderate, and high need. All mentees can complete the mentee needs checklist independently or in consultation with their mentor. By completing the checklist

Table 1.1 Mentee needs checklist

Directions: Rate the mentee in each of the following areas to determine areas of support.

Mentee Needs Checklist			
Areas of Support to Consider:	**High Need**	**Moderate Need**	**Low Need**
1. Assessing student progress.			
2. Making accommodations or modifications for students.			
3. Lesson planning ☑: long- ☐ or short-term ☐ plans.			
4. Writing goals and objectives.			
5. Writing IEPs.			
6. Completing paperwork related to district procedures.			
7. Setting up the classroom environment.			
8. Creating classroom rules.			
9. Enforcing classroom rules.			
10. Managing classroom instructional time or downtime.			
11. Locating and using grade-level expectations or state standards.			
12. Obtaining and locating classroom materials.			
13. Understanding testing materials and procedures.			
14. Ideas for teaching specific lessons.			
15. Organizing student papers and records.			
16. Learning more about the subject matter.			
17. Motivating students.			
18. Working with paraprofessionals.			
19. Working with parents.			
20. Collaborating with general education teachers.			
Total			
Priority Areas to Link to Action Plan			
1.		2.	
3.		4.	

together, the mentor and mentee can discuss critical areas of need and identify common goals. When completing the checklist independently, the mentor and mentee should meet to compare their perceptions and negotiate any differences. The goal of using the mentee needs checklist is to clarify the mentor and mentee's perceived areas of need and link them to the action plan (discussed later in this chapter).

Mentors play an important role in supporting new special education teachers. These diverse teachers will vary in their levels of need, from the teachers who are simply learning the school district's paperwork to those teachers who struggle in all areas and are trying to make it from one day to the next. Although the mentees' needs do vary, there are common needs of all new special education teachers, which are discussed next.

WHAT NEW SPECIAL EDUCATION TEACHERS NEED

Each Group of Teachers Will Have Varying Needs. Teachers in special education are faced with countless responsibilities ranging from instructional responsibilities, such as differentiating lesson plans, to compliance issues, such as writing IEPs that exceed ten pages. In addition, special education teachers work with diverse groups of students with varying instructional and social needs. Given these many challenges, the new special education teacher needs support and guidance from an experienced special education mentor to learn the explicit as well as hidden curriculum, or unwritten rules of the school (Whitaker, 2000a).

Richard Lavoie (1994), a well-known expert on learning disabilities, discusses the hidden curriculum as it relates to children with learning disabilities in his video, *Learning Disabilities and Social Skills: Last One Picked . . . First One Picked On.* The hidden curriculum consists of the unwritten rules of the school or environment that are not explicitly stated, but that everyone knows and follows. These rules are ones that students with learning disabilities have the most difficulty learning. Likewise, new special education teachers may need their mentor to teach them the hidden curriculum of the school. Perhaps the new teacher needs to know that one of the physical education teachers is more receptive to having mainstreamed students with behavior disorders than the other, or that if student materials are needed, it is easier to get them from the teacher next door rather than from the secretary who has the key to the bookroom. Teaching the new teacher about the hidden curriculum is one of many ways the mentor can support his or her mentee.

Common Needs. There is an emerging body of research on the types of supports new special education teachers need. Whitaker (2000a) conducted focus groups with beginning special education teachers and identified that they need support in the following areas: emotional support, system information related to the school or district, system information related to special education, materials or resources, discipline, curriculum or instruction, interaction with others, and management. Of these eight areas, teachers in the focus groups identified emotional support and system information as the most valuable

Table 1.2 Ways to provide emotional support

1. Listen.

2. Don't interrupt until the mentee is done talking.

3. Reaffirm the things the mentee is doing well.

4. Use clarifying statements to confirm you are listening. For example, "Your frustration seems to be mainly with Marc and Yolanda's behavior."

5. Avoid judging the mentee's actions.

6. If asked, provide suggestions.

supports to new teachers. In addition, the results from an initial survey (White & Mason, 2001a) of new teachers and mentors revealed that the types of support new special education teachers valued most were emotional support, ideas for teaching specific lessons, help to reduce frustration, and help to obtain classroom materials. Each type of support is discussed in further detail.

Emotional Support

Providing emotional support is important for mentors to consider when working with mentees because teaching can be an isolating profession (Gordon, 1991; Whitaker, 2000a). Many first-year special education teachers feel isolated, especially those teaching in a self-contained service delivery model or working without a paraeducator. Having a mentor that provides emotional support can help reduce these feelings of isolation. Kristie, one of the new teachers in our program wrote, "Being able to talk with my mentor was like taking a daily dose of medicine. It calmed my nerves and allowed me to realize that I was not the only teacher to encounter these difficulties." As discussed in Chapter 4, providing emotional support is part of the "assist not assess" philosophy of being a mentor. Mentees are not always looking for answers to their difficulties, but are in search of a person who understands their experience. A beginning teacher who just finished the school day and experienced the worst student behavior she ever encountered does not necessarily want solutions. She is looking for the comfort of a teacher who has been through the same or a similar experience and knows what she's feeling. Table 1.2 summarizes ways to provide emotional support to mentees.

Ideas for Specific Lessons

A second way for mentors to support mentees is to give them ideas for teaching specific lessons, a type of curricular support. The pairing of the mentor and mentee is critical for the success of curricular support. Ideally, mentors and mentees should have similar teaching assignments (Whitaker, 2001), or the mentor must have prior experience working in the same service delivery model with the same types of students as the mentee (Whitaker, 2000b). Obviously a mentor with ten years of experience teaching students with moderate intellectual disabilities would not be helpful for providing specific lesson ideas to a first-year teacher of students with learning disabilities. The first-year learning disabilities teacher should be paired with another teacher with the same experience or similar teaching assignment.

If the mentor does not have the same teaching assignment as the mentee, then he or she should be knowledgeable about resources to help provide specific ideas for the lesson. Perhaps the mentor or the mentoring program coordinator knows another learning disabilities teacher in a nearby school that the mentee could contact. The school district program specialist for learning disabilities may be a knowledgeable source for instructional ideas. The mentor may even refer the mentee to his or her favorite Internet site to locate specific ideas for teaching the lesson (White & Mason, 2001a) or suggest one of the Internet sites found in Table 1.3.

Another way to use technology to empower the mentee and provide specific ideas for lessons is to post the question about the instructional lesson on an Internet mentoring discussion board. The mentor and mentee can visit some of the Web sites listed in Table 1.4 that have interactive discussion boards. Discussion boards provide forums for discussion teaching ideas with individuals of diverse experiences from across the world. The mentees can read questions from other individuals as well as post their own questions about ideas for a lesson or instructional unit. Frequently checking the Web site for new responses becomes enjoyable and expands the mentee's professional network.

The mentor can also observe the mentee during instruction to gain ideas about the content they teach and to watch the way students interact independently and as a group. Direct observation of the students provides the mentor with information about group dynamics that influence his or her specific instructional recommendations. Some groups of students may not work well in cooperative groups, whereas others may. Based on the mentor's feedback, the special education teacher teaching the same instructional lesson to multiple groups of students can modify the lesson and teach it again to another group.

Time and scheduling constraints may make it difficult for the mentor and mentee to find time to do observations of each other. One solution may be to use videotaped teaching sessions as a springboard for discussions. The mentor can videotape him or herself teaching and share the tape with the mentee as part of a support activity. The mentor and mentee can review the tape together, and the mentor can "think aloud" about changes he or she would make. The mentees may feel uneasy taping themselves; however, the opportunity to watch yourself teach and reflect on how others view you is a powerful learning tool.

Additional curricular ideas for mentors are displayed in Table 1.5. Each of these ideas provides a launching point for helping the mentees respond to students' diverse curricular needs. Providing the mentee with specific curricular ideas for instruction can help reduce frustration.

Reducing Frustration

The mentee's first year of teaching is filled with many triumphs as well as frustrations (White & Mason, 2001a). There are several ways the mentor can support the mentee to reduce his or her common frustrations. For example, the mentor can help locate classroom materials, provide the needed paperwork and

Table 1.3 Online resources for lesson planning

Online Resources for Lessons				
	Elementary School	**Middle School**	**High School**	**Comments**
Reading/ Literacy	http://www.awesomelibrary.org/special-ed.html			Special education lesson plans for teachers
	http://www.getreadytoread.org/skillE.cfm		N/A	Elementary and middle school reading lessons
	http://www.interventioncentral.com			Provides detailed strategies to increase phonics skills, reading decoding, fluency, and comprehension
Mathematics	http://teams.lacoe.edu/documentation/places/lessons.html			Math plans for special and general education
	http://www.teachnology.com/teachers/lesson_plans/			Lesson plans for math and all subjects
Science	http://k-6educators.about.com/cs/science/			Science lesson plans—searchable
	http://www.lessonplanspage.com/Science.htm			Plans for all grades
Social Studies	http://www.teachers.net/cgi-bin/lessons/sort.cgi?searchterm=Social+Studies			Social studies ideas—all grades
	N/A	http://7-12educators.about.com/cs/socialstudies/		Plans for middle and high school
Resources in Spanish	http://paidos.rediris.es/needirectorio/			Resources for teachers and parents

forms for notifying parents about IEP meetings, and assist with writing the IEP (White & Mason, 2001b). Additionally, many mentors provide their mentee with a contact list of people in the building or school district with their phone numbers, e-mail addresses, and role (see Table 1.6). Chris, a graduate of a teacher preparation program and a first-year special education teacher, was

Table 1.4   Internet mentoring discussion boards

Web Address	Site Description
http://www.dyslexia-teacher.com/t98.html	The Dyslexia Teacher Web site has a discussion board and resources on dyslexia
http://www.inspiringteachers.com/mentoring/boards.html	Beginning Teacher's Toolbox contains a discussion board
http://www.teachers.net/chat/	This is the teachers.net Web site, which contains a discussion board and resources for all teaching disciplines
http://www.epals.com/tools/forum/	ePALS has a discussion board related to technology use
http://www.coe.fau.edu/cspd/discussion/	Special education discussion board from a regional personnel development site

Table 1.5   Specific curriculum ideas

Curriculum Concerns: Ideas for Mentors
Share copies of your units and student projects.
Co-plan a lesson built around the general education curriculum standards.
Show the mentee how to make accommodations to a lesson.
Show the mentee how you identify a student's learning style.
Model successful teaching techniques in their classroom.
Show the mentee how to order specific curriculum materials you find useful.
Show the mentee how to design and set up instructional learning centers.

frustrated that he had four computers in his classroom, and only one worked. He explained, "The computer is such a powerful teaching tool, and to have them sitting like oversize paperweights was driving me up the wall. Thankfully my mentor knew the person to call that gets things done, and within two weeks the computers were up and running." If Chris had to track down the school district's systems support personnel, it would have taken him weeks because most of his planning period time was spent grading papers, contacting parents, and preparing for his next class. Although broken computers may not frustrate some teachers, Chris looked at the computer area several times a day and each time felt the frustration. His mentor helped reduce this frustration, which permitted Chris to focus on implementing the computer center.

Table 1.6   Resource contact list

Resource Contact List			
Position	**Name**	**Phone Number**	**E-mail Address**
Principal			
Assistant Principal			
Guidance Counselor			
Secretary			
Bookkeeper			
Office Staff			
Speech Therapist			
Occupational Therapist			
Physical Therapist			
School Nurse			
Paraprofessional			
Head Custodian			
Cafeteria Food Staff			
Cafeteria Monitor			
Audio-Visual Contact			
Technology Specialist			
Staffing/Program Specialist			
District Special Education Director			
School Psychologist			
Crisis Counselor			
Social Worker			
Afterschool Program Coordinator			
Bus Driver			
Other			
Other			

Table 1.7   Surveying and solving frustrations

Copy this form and keep it on your desk. When you experience a frustration, write it down so that later you can later discuss it with your mentor.

Frustration	Potential Solution or Resource
1.	
2.	
3.	
4.	
5.	
6.	
7.	
8.	
9.	
10.	

New special education teachers will feel frustrated by a variety of things such as the amount of time it takes to copy materials, complete paperwork, or simply learn how to use the school's automated telephone system. One way to help the mentee identify and remember their frustrations is to use the Solving Frustrations Survey located in Table 1.7. Oftentimes the mentee becomes engrossed in an activity or instructional lesson and later forgets the frustrating circumstances. If the mentee writes a few words as a reminder about what occurred, he or she can later discuss solutions with a mentor.

Systems Support and Information Relating to the School or District

Initially, the mentor spends considerable time explaining school district paperwork, policies, and procedures to the mentee. New special education teachers quickly realize that each school district has different procedures for completing paperwork and complying with state and federal regulations. New special education teachers coming from another school district and recent graduates of teacher preparation programs understand special education vocabulary and have the knowledge to write IEPs. Mentors can provide this

Table 1.8   Paperwork scavenger hunt

Directions: Locate all required forms. Create a file or notebook section for each set of forms according to use (e.g., behavioral forms, parent notification forms, IEP forms, etc.).

Form Name*	Form Use	Form Number	Blank Form Location
Parent Notification of Meeting			
Consent for Evaluation			
Student Study Team Conference Notes			
IEP Forms			
Transition Planning Form			
Notification of Reevaluation			
Initial Placement Form			
Reevaluation Summary Form			
Functional Assessment Form			
Behavior Intervention Plan			
Interim Progress Reports			

*Form names will vary from district to district; these are sample form names.

group with additional knowledge of the specific policies and procedures of the school district. Mentors working with new special education teachers without any educational training will have to provide extensive knowledge of special education vocabulary, paperwork, and procedures. In a recent survey of special education mentors, weekly time commitments ranged from 15 minutes to 4 hours depending on the needs of the mentee (White & Mason, 2001a).

One of the most time-consuming tasks for mentors and mentees is completing necessary paperwork. To expedite the paperwork explanation process, the mentor and mentee can locate copies of all required school district paperwork using the paperwork scavenger hunt located in Table 1.8. By completing the paperwork scavenger hunt activity, the mentee can create a file or notebook with completed samples of all required paperwork. For example, the mentee can create files for parent notifications, referrals, IEPs, behavior intervention plans, and functional behavior assessments. The location of additional blank forms should be noted on the paperwork scavenger hunt so the mentee knows if he or she should look in the school office, on an Internet site, or in the district office.

As a collaborative activity, the mentor and mentee can complete a set of paperwork in each area based on a child in the classroom. Although this activity may be time-consuming, it provides the mentee with a guide for completing all forms using the required format. The mentee can refer to these forms all year as a model for paperwork completion. Ideally, a student requiring a new IEP or functional assessment of behavior is chosen to make the activity worthy of the time required for completion. The mentor could give the mentee copies of all of his or her completed forms; however, jointly completing the forms teaches, rather than only shows, the mentee what to do and enhances information retention. Sylvia Ostbye, a prekindergarten special education teacher explained:

> I provided Amy [her mentee] with many activities and ideas that I collected and tried over many years. I also tutored her on the writing of IEPs using the computer program currently being used by our county and I helped her write the first one. Amy caught on quickly and her IEPs were terrific.

With direct instruction from her mentor on writing an IEP for a student, Amy learned the district format and quickly became independent.

Additional ideas for mentors to use when acquainting the mentees to the school environment are located in Table 1.9. Although some of these ideas may appear commonsense, they are supported by research and help send a message of welcoming and belonging that can be comforting to a new special education teacher (Pardini, 2002). William, a new special education teacher commented,

> When Laura [the mentor] took me around to meet all the teachers and support staff, it made me feel valued and implied that I was a team member. I felt an instant belonging to the school family.

Table 1.9   School environment concerns

School Environment Concerns: Ideas for Mentors
Introduce the mentee to school faculty and staff.
Show the mentee how to locate needed materials.
Help the mentee learn the shortcuts of the building's physical design.
Explain supervisory tasks (e.g., bus duty, student pickup, hall monitor between classes).
Show the mentee how to request or make photocopies of materials.
Explain how to request a substitute teacher when the mentee is absent.
Explain the attitudes of other teachers.

If William's mentor had not personally introduced him to the faculty and staff, it could have taken him several weeks to individually meet everyone, and he may have felt professionally isolated. Often times the smallest gestures create the largest impact.

The specific supports of emotional support, specific curricular ideas, reducing frustrations, and systems support were identified by new special education teachers as the most important components for a successful first year of teaching (White & Mason, 2001a; Whitaker, 2000a). These supports represent variables new special education teacher found valuable. In addition to these, special education teachers also rate many other types of supports as valuable. Additional specific special education supports, such as instructional strategies, accommodations, and classroom management are discussed in Chapter 2.

SUPPORTS ESE MENTORS CAN PROVIDE MENTEES

As noted previously, there are numerous specific supports that mentors can provide mentees. However, these supports will vary depending on the individual needs of each mentee. Of primary importance for the mentor is prioritizing the mentee's most important needs. The mentor will need to assess the mentee's current level of functioning to identify any specific needs using an activity such as the one in Table 1.1. The mentee needs checklist can be completed independently or collaboratively, and after the mentee's primary needs are identified, they can be incorporated into an action plan. The action plan helps the mentee identify and make progress toward enhancing his or her teaching skills (see Resource A).

An action plan is not an evaluative instrument. It is a collaboratively designed document used for the benefit of the mentee and mentor to focus on common goals, define responsibilities, and chronicle the mentee's professional progress. Additionally, the action plan is a working document that is revised and modified as needed. The mentor and mentee should review the action plan monthly. The primary components of the action plan are (a) identifying goals, (b) identifying objectives, (c) creating specific steps to accomplish the objectives, and (d) evaluating the outcome and using the information learned. Although each component is discussed individually for the purpose of discussion, each component is interrelated.

The initial step of the action plan is to identify goals the mentee wants to accomplish. The action plan in Resource A contains space to write up to four goals. The goals may relate to the mentee's curricular, behavioral, personal, or other needs. Perhaps the mentee desires to increase the average math score of his students, decrease the number of times students call out for assistance, or learn how to reduce the amount of time required for grading student work. Some goals selected by the mentor and mentee may address the overwhelming amount of paperwork associated with being a special education teacher. They may want to look for ways to streamline administrative activities for a new teacher. Similar to writing annual goals on a student's IEP, goals on the mentor-mentee action plan should be linked to assessment and based on need. When the pair select the goals for the year, they must keep in mind that some goals escalate teacher performance pressure, and some serve to de-escalate the pressure. The math curriculum workshop may be necessary, but putting it off until the summer may de-escalate pressure on the new teacher. The mentor's judgment will be essential in determining the priority of the goals.

As mentioned previously, the Mentee Needs Checklist, Table 1.1, is one technique the mentee and mentor may collaboratively use to identify needs. Other suggestions for identifying the mentee's primary needs are using an informal discussion and answering the question, What aspect of my teaching do I want to improve? The assessment can also be based on needs identified by the mentor while observing the mentee's classroom teaching. Remember that whichever technique is used to identify the goal(s), the goal(s) must be valued as important by the mentee. It is not sufficient for the mentor to identify a goal as important and list it on the action plan without the mentee holding the same belief. The mentee must recognize the goal as valuable to expend effort accomplishing it.

Once the goal is identified, the second component is writing objectives in measurable terms to adequately measure progress. The example completed action in Resource A refers to the second component as the "What." The "What" component is a statement of what the mentee wants to accomplish. For example, the objective "The mentee will increase the use of specific academic praise" is not written specifically enough to document progress. However, the objective is measurable when stated, "The mentee will increase the use of specific academic praise to a minimum of ten times during a one-hour lesson." Measurable goals and objectives facilitate the documentation of progress and are more useful to the mentee and mentor.

The third step of the action plan is the "So What" component. This component contains information regarding specific steps the mentee will take to accomplish his or her objectives. The mentee may ask him or herself, "So what action must I take to accomplish this objective?" If the mentee's goal is to increase the use of specific academic praise to a minimum of ten times during a one-hour lesson, the mentee and mentor may brainstorm a list of potential solutions. Example solutions to this objective may include (a) posting a visual cue in the classroom, (b) setting a timer to sound every ten minutes, and (c) audiotaping a lesson and replaying it after school to count the number of specific academic praises. From the list, the mentee and mentor may decide what the first action is, posting a visual cue in the classroom followed by audio-taping a lesson.

The "So What" actions may be responsibilities of the mentee, mentor, or other individual. In the aforementioned specific academic praise example, the mentee completed all actions. If the mentee's second objective was related to a student's behavioral need, the mentee and mentor may both take action. For example, the mentee's second objective is to reduce the number of verbal outbursts from a student from five to one per day. The mentee and mentor may decide to work together to accomplish this objective. Upon the mentee identifying the student's signs of frustration, such as wrinkling his brow, clutching his fists, and having deep sighs, she will ask the student to deliver a note to the mentor's classroom. This activity diffuses the student's frustration and permits him to regain his focus. At the same time, it allows the mentee to achieve her objective of decreasing the student's verbal outbursts to no more than one per day.

The last component of the action plan is to evaluate and reflect on the outcome. This component is termed "Now What?" During this component, the mentee and mentor examine the data and ask the question, Now that we have the data, what should we do? Various answers come to mind when this question is posed. Assuming the mentee is now providing at least ten specific academic praises each hour, he may decide to remove the visual cue from the classroom. Perhaps the mentee will decide to monitor his specific academic praise in another class or with another group of students to see if his behavior generalizes to new environments. During this component, the mentee and mentor have the ability to reflect on what went well and discuss any future changes. Of course if the outcome documents successful completion of the objective and goal, the mentee may decide to focus on a new goal. If the outcome does not meet expectations, the mentee will likely refine the action steps or decide to try a new activity.

Overall, the action plan helps provide support and a central focus for chronicling the mentee's professional growth. Ultimately it is up to the mentoring pair to recognize the value of an action plan because the plan becomes as useful and valuable as the mentee and mentor desire. Clearly the action plan has no value if it is created but remains filed. On the other hand, if the action plan becomes a central conversational component for the mentor and mentee to use as a reflection tool, the action plan becomes pivotal. By having an action plan, the new special education teacher feels supported and many of his or her fears and anxieties subside.

Note of caution: Do not let this action plan become an evaluation instrument for the administration. This is between the mentor and mentee alone. It should not be factored into the annual evaluation, merit pay, or annual assessment of the new teacher.

FEARS AND ANXIETIES OF NEW TEACHERS

All new special education teachers have concerns associated with their first year of teaching. Like most human behaviors, new teachers' fears and anxieties can be represented by a bell-shaped curve such as the normal distribution curve. As illustrated in Figure 1.1, about 68% of new special education teachers have relatively the same level of anxiety: the middle section of the normal distribution curve. Approximately another 15% of teachers experience little anxiety and have above-average confidence in their teaching abilities: the far right side of the curve. The final 15% of teachers will feel less confident about their abilities and experience higher than normal levels of anxiety: represented by the far left side of the curve. Although there are varying degrees of concerns that new special education teachers experience, the issues which cause anxiety are similar. The most common fears and anxieties of new special education teachers' experience include issues such as time management, workload, instruction, collaboration, accountability, motivating students, and

Figure 1.1 Anxiety levels of new special education teachers

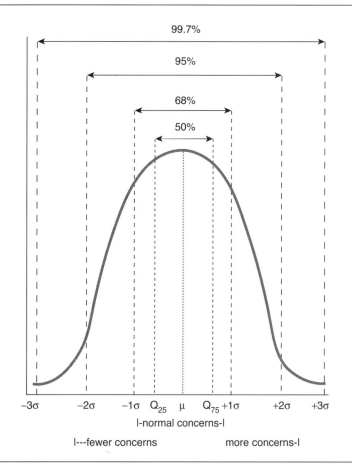

professional isolation (White & Mason, 2001a; Wilson, Ireton, & Wood, 1997; Zabel & Zabel, 2001).

This graph shows the percentage of teacher concerns and fears as represented by a bell-shaped curve.

Researchers from the Council for Exceptional Children's Mentoring Induction Project (White & Mason, 2001) identified the most urgent concerns of new teachers as time management, workload, providing instruction, and collaborating with general educators and parents. Additional areas of concern for new teachers also include technology, accountability, cultural awareness, motivation of students, and isolation. The mentor has a critical role working to support the mentee in each of these areas. Given the high level of importance to successful teacher induction, each area is discussed in depth in Chapter 5.

SCHOOL ADMINISTRATOR'S ROLE

Up to this point, the narrative has primarily focused on ways mentors can support the mentee. The school principal or school administrator is another valuable support for the mentee (Boyer & Lee, 2001). New special education teachers feel increased emotional support and less social and professional

isolation with a supportive administrator (Bridges to Success, 2003). By supporting the special education teacher, the school administrator sends the message that they have a vested interest in the teacher and concern for their success. Additionally, administrators value that supporting new special education teachers promotes teacher retention and creates less teacher turnover in their schools. Teachers feel disconnected from the school climate without administrator support. A lack of administrator support is one frequently cited reason new special education teachers leave the classroom (Bridges to Success, 2003; Miller, Brownell, & Smith, 1999).

In addition to supporting the new special education teacher, the school administrator has a substantial influence on the role and assignment of the mentee (Boyer & Lee, 2001) as well as the formal evaluation of the mentee's teaching performance. The building administrator has the responsibility of formally documenting the mentee's teaching performance. As recommended by White and Mason (2001b) in their Council for Exceptional Children Mentoring Induction Project, mentors should not be placed in a position to formally evaluate their mentees. Lloyd, Wood, & Moreno (2000) also recommend that the mentor is a facilitator, not an evaluator. If the mentor is placed in the role of evaluator, it dramatically changes the mentor-mentee relationship from supportive to supervisory. No longer is the mentor viewed as a confidant, but rather as a performance evaluator. If the mentor is asked to provide evaluative data on the mentee, regardless whether the mentee is doing well or poor, he or she should politely decline the request by citing that such a disclosure is not in the best interest of the mentee or mentor. Providing evaluative data about the mentee sabotages the mentor's efforts to develop and maintain a collegial relationship with his or her mentee.

ASSIGNMENT OF NEW TEACHERS

There are two types of assignments related to new special education teachers that have important implications for a successful year. The first assignment is the new teacher's teaching assignment made by the school administrator. Second is the assignment of the mentor to the mentee, another decision typically made by the school administrator.

Teacher Assignment

For better or worse, most experienced teachers remember their first year of teaching. The first year of teaching is one that typically contains numerous trials and tribulations as new teachers learn the ins and outs of their profession. Of particular importance during the first year of teaching is the teaching assignment (Griffin, Winn, Otis-Wilborn, & Kilgore, 2003). The beginning special education teacher's assignment can either make or break his or her first year of teaching. Fortunately, most new teachers receive fair teaching assignments during their first year; some do not. Some new special education teachers will be assigned to classrooms without adequate furniture, materials, space, or supplies. Other teachers will have a roster of students with a history of being problematic or get assigned the largest roster of students.

As the new special education teacher, and a male, Lorenzo's principal felt he would be able to handle the boys with behavior disorders, so he assigned all five to his cross-categorical elementary classroom. At the end of his first year of teaching, Lorenzo commented, "This [assignment] was unfair. Because I was the new teacher, I was stuck with the students with the lowest academics and most challenging behaviors."

More challenging assignments, like Lorenzo's, may leave many new teachers feeling apprehensive and questioning their preparedness during the first weeks of the school year. Unfortunately, Lorenzo's situation happens to many new special education teachers who receive the most challenging students and often the least amount of materials. According to Carl D. Glickman, "In most professions, the challenge of the job increases over time as one acquires experience and expertise. In teaching, we've had it reversed. Typically, the most challenging situation a teacher experienced was in his or her first year" (Glickman, quoted in Whitaker, 2001). With careful consideration, the school administrator can help ensure that all teachers' assignments reflect equity in the student distribution and the availability of classroom materials.

School administrators have the crucial role of ensuring that the new special education teacher does not complete his or her first year of teaching under the unfavorable conditions as previously noted. Teaching in an unsupportive environment during the first year may cause the new special education teacher to question his or her teaching skills as well as contemplate leaving the profession (Whitaker, 2001). New special education teachers, depending on their background, will question their skills in different areas such as planning instruction, meeting diverse needs of students, managing student behavior, or working with other professionals. One way the school administrator can help support and retain new special education teachers is to provide a wonderful assignment and favorable teaching conditions. A second way the school administrator can retain new special education teachers is to assign an effective mentor.

Mentor Assignment

The mentor is typically selected from the best of the profession. The "teacher of teachers" is who we all strive to be like. They are widely acknowledged as being good at their job or skilled professionals. This can set up a difficult situation for principals or those who determine the teachers' schedules and responsibilities. Should the best teachers be assigned additional duties that take away from their greatest skills? Many times the best teachers and managers are given difficult students with which to work because the administration knows they can do the job. An administrator has to consider the amount of attention a new teacher may demand from a mentor. In considering the task demands of mentoring, the administrator may assign the mentor to a lightened teaching schedule, or a schedule that allows for some flexibility in timing (i.e., the mentor and mentee have a shared planning time). The assignment of the new special education teacher to a mentor is one important decision that impacts every area of the mentoring relationship. In a review of studies on new teacher induction in special education, Griffin et al. (2003) confirm that both mentors and mentees should be special educators. In their study on mentoring support, Lloyd et al. (2000) also note that the principal is the individual primarily responsible for the selection of mentors. Ideally, the school principal should consult with the mentor teacher before making an assignment to assess his or her willingness to mentor as well as their perceived "fit" with the mentee. If the principal's school district works with any universities to implement new teacher induction mentoring programs, the principal may utilize them as a resource for selecting a mentor because the mentor does not have to teach at the same school as the mentee. Preferably, the mentor and mentee would both teach students of similar disabilities and be in the same school. In special education this does not always occur, and often there are only one or two special education teachers in the entire school: one for mild disabilities and one for moderate and severe disabilities. Whitaker (2000b) recommends that the first priority in selecting a mentor should be to pair a mentor and mentee who teach students with similar disabilities. When this is not possible, she recommends a co-mentoring arrangement wherein the mentee has two mentor teachers: one in the building to provide emotional support, socialization into the school culture, etc.; and one mentor who can mentor the special education issues of teaching. The mentor in the same school as the mentee can provide unscheduled meetings, the most frequently experienced form of support (Whitaker, 2000b). The mentor and mentee in different schools can use scheduled or unscheduled times to communicate by utilizing technologies such as e-mail, Internet video cameras, and the telephone. These technologies can assist the mentor and mentee in communicating when the need arises. Whitaker reports that mentor teachers reported scheduled meetings second in support and effectiveness in meeting the mentee's needs.

To assess the effectiveness of the mentoring relationship, the principal should regularly obtain feedback from the mentor and mentee. When the mentor and mentee roles are clearly defined (see Chapter 3 for roles of both the mentor and the mentee), assessing the relationship becomes clearer for the building administrator. Clearly defined roles and responsibilities remove any ambiguity from tasks the mentor and mentee should accomplish. If the administrator, mentee, or mentor feel the relationship is not beneficial, opportunities for change and making another assignment should be permitted. Table 1.10 provides administrators with specific ideas for supporting the mentee.

School administrators should keep in mind that some new teachers are hesitant to admit that they lack the materials or resources with which to teach because they worry it will make them look unprepared. Some mentees believe that asking for help is a sign of weakness. By being aware of these needs, the school administrator takes a proactive approach toward supporting new special education teachers before any problematic issues arise. Additional supports for beginning special education teachers are discussed in Chapter 2.

Table 1.10   Administrator support for the new special education teacher

	Administrator Suggestions for Helping New Special Education Teachers
1.	Carefully contemplate the mentor-mentee match.
2.	Network out of your own school to locate mentor teachers by contacting other principals or the school district special education director.
3.	Assign the new special education teacher a room in the building, not a portable.
4.	Provide funding for the new teacher to purchase supplies.
5.	Ensure enough books and supplies were ordered for the new special education teacher.
6.	Check with the new teacher during the first few days of school to see if the teacher has supplies: copies of teacher's manuals, curriculum guides (including those for the general education curriculum).
7.	Provide adequate paraprofessional support.
8.	Create a supportive climate such as having an open-door office policy.
9.	Follow through with consistent disciplining of students.
10.	Allow shared decision making by the new teacher and school staff.
11.	Provide release time so the new special education teacher can observe other teachers, meet with his or her mentor, and attend professional development trainings.
12.	Establish a close working relationship by observing without forms and attending IEP meetings with the new special education teacher.
13.	Reduce the mentee and mentor noninstructional responsibilities such as bus or cafeteria duty and committee membership.
14.	Participate in evaluating the mentoring program and making improvements.
15.	Set up a schedule for conducting formal observations of the mentee.
16.	After the observation, provide clear feedback and specific suggestions to the new special education teacher.
17.	Continually share information targeted to new special education teachers.

WHAT IF?

The newest special education teacher in your school is a "real go-getter." She is an active participant at faculty meetings, participates in the faculty discussions, and seems to have it all together. The tradition at your school is to match new teachers with a mentor. In your role as program administrator, you talked with the new teacher about the mentoring program. She told you she didn't need a mentor. What do you do?

Possible Solutions Include

Assign a mentor to work with the new teacher anyway, but talk with both the mentor and mentee explaining that the mentor is available to the mentee to help with all sorts of school issues. The mentor is there to help whenever the mentee needs him or her. Who knows, the mentee may need information further into the school year, and the mentor would be an excellent resource for issues beyond special education.

Internet Sites on Mentoring

- Teacher.Net Mentor Center: http://teachers.net/mentors/
- Teacher Mentoring: www.coled.mankato.msus.edu/dept/labdist/mentor/
- ASCD Mentoring Resources: www.mentors.net
- Best Practices in Mentoring: www.teachermentors.com
- Bridges to Success Special Education Teacher Induction: www.tr.wou. edu
- Council for Exceptional Children Mentoring Induction Principles and Guidelines: www.cec.sped.org/spotlight/udl/mip_g_manual_11pt.pdf

REFERENCES

Boyer, L., & Lee, C. (2001). Converting challenge to success: Supporting a new teacher of students with autism. *Journal of Special Education, 35*(2), 75–83.

Bridges to Success. (2003). Guidelines for special education administrator support. Retrieved May 6, 2003, from http://www.tr.wou.edu/bridges2/sped_support.htm

Council for Exceptional Children. (2001). *Bright futures for exceptional learners.* Reston, VA: Author.

Feiman-Nesmer, S. (1996). *Teacher mentoring: A critical review.* (Report No. EDO-SP-95–2). Washington, DC: Office of Educational Research and Improvement. (ERIC Document Reproduction Service No. ED397060).

Gordon, S. P. (1991). *How to help beginning teachers succeed.* Alexandria, VA: Association for Supervision and Curriculum Development.

Griffin, C. C., Winn, J. A., Otis-Wilborn, A., & Kilgore, K. L. (2003). *New teacher induction in special education.* Retrieved August 6, 2003, from www.coe.ufl.edu/coppse/

Lavoie, R. D. (1994). *Learning disabilities and social skills: Last one picked . . . first one picked on.* Washington, DC: WETA PBS Video.

Lloyd, S. R., Wood, T. A., & Moreno, G. (2000). What's a mentor to do? *Teaching Exceptional Children, 33*(1), 38–42.

Mason, C., & White, M. (2001). The mentoring induction project: Supporting new teachers—hints for mentors and mentoring coordinators. *Teaching Exceptional Children, 34*(1), 80–81.

Miller, M. D., Brownell, M. T., & Smith, S. W. (1999). Factors that predict teachers staying in, leaving, or transferring from the special education classroom. *Exceptional Children, 65*(2), 201–218.

Pardini, P. (2002). Stitching new teachers into the school's fabric. *Journal of Staff Development, 23*(3), 23–26.

U.S. Department of Education. (2002). *No Child Left Behind.* Washington, DC: Author. Retrieved from http://www.ed.gov/nclb/landing.jhtml#

Whitaker, S. D. (2000a). What do first-year special education teachers need? *Teaching Exceptional Children, 33*(1), 28–36.

Whitaker, S. D. (2000b). Mentoring beginning special education teachers and the relationship to attrition. *Exceptional Children, 66*(4), 546–566.

Whitaker, S. D. (2001). Supporting beginning special education teachers. *Focus on Exceptional Children, 34*(4), 1–18.

White, M., & Mason, C. (2001a). New teacher supports. *Teaching Exceptional Children, 33*(3), 91.

White, M., & Mason, C. (2001b). The mentoring induction project: What new teachers need from mentors. *Teaching Exceptional Children, 33*(6), 81.

Wilson, B., Ireton, J., & Wood, J. A. (1997). Beginning teacher fears. *Education, 117*(3), 396–400.

Zabel, R. H., & Zabel, M. K. (2001). Revisiting burnout among special education teachers: Do age, experience, and preparation still matter? *Teacher Education and Special Education, 24*(2), 128–139.

Supports for Special Education Teachers 2

VIGNETTE

Being an educator and loving what I do, I have always been more than willing to help any teacher. This year the teacher who took the prekindergarten special education classroom position was from out-of-state and was out-of-field. I was asked to complete a formal training to become her mentor as requested by my school administrator. The district-led training was wonderful because it taught me how to effectively communicate using listening and reflective questioning. The training also provided me with the characteristics of new special education teachers and their needs. This was extremely valuable because as a traditionally trained teacher, my background and training differed from out-of-field teachers. I quickly realized that a lot of the basic special education information that I took for granted may be new to the out-of-field teacher. Through this training, and working with my mentee, I have grown immensely as a person and an educator. It made me rethink what we do as special education teachers. My mentee's growth was a compliment to me and the relationship we developed.

—Nicki O'Neill

A school district's support program for new special education teachers can make the difference between a teacher remaining or leaving their school district or teaching position. Special education teachers that are supported by colleagues and school district personnel are better prepared to cope with the challenges associated with being a new teacher. The need for quality special education mentoring programs is clear and the Council for Exceptional Children (CEC) (2003) provides five goals for special education mentorship programs:

1. Facilitating the application of knowledge and skills learned

2. Conveying advanced knowledge and skills

3. Acculturating into the school's learning community

4. Reducing job stress and enhancing job satisfaction

5. Supporting professional induction (p. 13)

According to the Council for Exceptional Children, "The purpose of mentors is to provide expertise and support to teachers on a continuing basis for at least the first year of practice in that area of licensure" (p. 13). Additionally, they recommend that the mentor should be experienced in the same or similar role as the mentee. The Council for Exceptional Children's recommended goals have been integrated throughout each chapter of this book. The summarized CEC goals are located in Resource B. The primary purposes of this chapter are to provide special education mentors with tools they can use when working with mentees and to explain how mentors can become a useful professional resource.

UNIQUENESS OF SPECIAL EDUCATION

Special education teachers encounter issues that are unique to education. These issues, such as the Individuals With Disabilities Education Act legislation (IDEA), various forms of student assessment (alternate, norm-referenced, criterion, curriculum-based, etc.), and children with medical issues can seem overwhelming to new special education teachers. The mentor is one of the primary people to help new special education teachers understand these complexities. Think back to your first year of teaching. How long did it take you to write your first individualized education plan (IEP)? Now think about how much faster you can write an IEP today. The time is probably much shorter today than during your first year of teaching. During my first year of teaching, my mentor gave me one of her well-written IEPs. I clearly remember studying her IEP as I wrote a draft of my first IEP. It was a time-consuming process even with her great IEP for use as a guide. Without her guide, I would have been quite frustrated. The process of learning new tasks is what new special education teachers encounter on a daily basis. As their mentor, your support is invaluable in teaching them about the intricacies of special education.

Some of the uniqueness of special education discussed in our book includes programmatic compliance, due process, IEPs, referrals, instructional strategies, making accommodations, and collaborating with general educators, parents, and paraeducators. These are some of the issues with which new special education teachers may need the most support. In addition to these types of supports, another valuable aid that mentors' provide is emotional support. Each type of support is discussed later; resources for mentors and mentees are provided.

Programmatic Compliance. New special education teachers enter their first year of teaching in the survival mode, focused on getting from day to day, so they may not be aware of the complexities related to programmatic compliance. From the exceptional student education director's point of view, having the special education program in compliance with federal and state regulations is paramount. One of the primary reasons the special education program must be in compliance with the laws is funding. A school district's special education federal and state monies can be reduced if they are not in compliance with all laws. Additionally, the school district faces large legal fees if they have to go to court over not providing services or appropriate opportunities for students with disabilities.

Due Process, IEPs, Referrals. The area of programmatic compliance of most concern to new special education teachers is the IEP. Each student's IEP must be written to conform to district standards and include all components as required by federal law. Mentees should write each IEP accurately and strongly enough to withstand the scrutiny of a lawyer during a due process hearing. I like to tell my special education student teachers to write their IEPs so that if they are ever legally challenged about a student's progress, they can defend themselves with an IEP that adheres to the law.

Many of the new special education teachers we work with experience the most difficulty writing IEPs with measurable annual goals and short-term objectives. Without having a measurable goal or objective, it is impossible to know if and when the student meets that objective. One new special education teacher wrote, "Rachelle will increase the knowledge of her reading skills." As you can tell, this annual goal is impossible to measure. After talking with the new special education teacher the annual goal she intended was, "Rachelle will increase her reading comprehension scores by six months as measured by the Woodcock Johnson Tests of Achievement." Mentors can use Table 2.1 with mentees to discuss and practice writing measurable annual goals and short-term objectives.

Other specific areas of the IEP that need to be in compliance are special education services, related services, supplemental aids and services, participation in general education, accommodations or modifications, and statewide testing. Fortunately, the new special education teacher has resource personnel at many levels to help ensure the IEP is properly written. The mentor is the individual at the school level who can help the mentee identify what the expected responses are for each of the areas within an IEP. Every school district has IEP nuances that are rarely addressed in teacher training programs.

In addition to his or her mentor, the mentee has the local education agency (LEA) representative, one or more school district–level compliance specialists, and the state department of education compliance contact to assist in answering compliance questions. As a new special education teacher just learning procedures, we recommend mentees ask a lot of questions rather than risk being out of

Table 2.1   Writing goals and objectives

The three required components in any annual goal or short term objective are	
1. **Conditions**–Conditions describe what or how the student will perform a task.	*Examples* (a) Given a math sheet with twenty single-digit addition problems . . . (b) Given a case of canned food . . . (c) Given a blank map of the United States . . .
2. **Behavior**–A measurable verb that describes the student's action.	(a) . . . Michael will correctly solve the problems . . . (b) . . . Zach will align them on the store shelves . . . (c) . . . Yolanda will match the name with each state . . .
3. **Criteria**–The percentage or way to measure the student's progress.	(a) . . . with 90% accuracy. (b) . . . nine out of ten times. (c) . . . with 80% accuracy.

Examples:

Given a math sheet with twenty single-digit addition problems, Michael will correctly solve the problems with 90% accuracy.

Given a case of canned food, Zach will neatly align the case of food on the store shelves nine out of ten times.

Given a blank map of the United States, Yolanda will match the name with the state with 80% accuracy.

Practice writing your own annual goal and short-term objectives:

(a)

(b)

(c)

compliance during an audit or enduring legal action from parents. Mentors can complete the Program Compliance Resource List found in Table 2.2 for mentees to use as a reference when they have a compliance question. In addition, mentors should take time to review their mentee's initial IEPs and discuss whether they are written in compliance with current laws.

At some schools, the new special education teachers may be the only faculty members in special education. In other schools there may be several special education faculty members. New special education teachers will be part of the child study team (also called student support team; student success team; problem solving team) process to discuss struggling students and implement

Table 2.2   Program compliance resources

Program Compliance Resource List	
Location & Name	Phone and E-mail
Department of Education Contact	
School District Contact 1	
School District Contact 2	
School-Based Administrator Contact (LEA)	
School-Based Teacher Contact	
Other	

supports prior to a special education referral. Mentors can support their mentees through this process by ensuring that they understand and can articulate the school district's referral process. Table 2.3 contains a referral flow diagram that mentors and mentees can complete to discuss how a child is referred for services. In addition, mentors can complete the flow diagram to show how the mentee refers a struggling child in their special education classroom.

> During Heather Hartog's first year as new special education teacher, she had to refer several of her students to the child study team because she felt they were not placed in the appropriate classrooms. As a result of her referrals, two of her students were placed in general education classrooms full-time.

Although Heather's results may differ from yours, many new special education teachers question the placement of one or more of their students.

In addition to referring their own students to the child study team, the new special education teacher may be asked by general education teachers to informally observe their struggling students as part of the child study team process. The mentee can draw upon his or her training and suggest strategies and ideas that the general education teacher can try with the student. The general education teacher can document the use of these strategies as prereferral interventions. Once the prereferral interventions are complete, the child study team can evaluate the results and determine whether the child needs a complete special education evaluation.

> Mentors should locate a copy of the Special Policies and Procedures (SP&P) manual for their mentee.

The mentor should make sure their mentee has a copy of the school district's special policies and procedures handbook, which in special education is commonly called the SP&P. The SP&P contains the complete guidelines for making special education referrals as well as the eligibility criteria used to determine whether students qualify for special education.

Table 2.3   Referral process

Student Referral/Child Study Team Steps
_____ School District

STEP 1: _____

⇩

STEP 2: _____

⇩

STEP 3: _____

⇩

STEP 4: _____

⇩

STEP 5: _____

⇩

STEP 6: _____

⇩

STEP 7: _____

⇩

STEP 8: _____

⇩

STEP 9: _____

⇩

STEP 10: _____

⇩

STEP 11: _____

⇩

STEP 12: _____

⇩

STEP 13: _____

⇩

STEP 14: _____

⇩

STEP 15: _____

Instructional Strategies. Numerous instructional strategies are used in special education. One current focus in education is on using scientifically or research validated instructional strategies with students. There is a great detail of support for teachers to use validated approaches to increase the performance and educational outcomes of students with disabilities. The exceptional student education director, a curriculum specialist, or the individual teacher often makes selection of an instructional strategy or curriculum. Mentors support new special education teachers by offering advice about which instructional strategies are appropriate for their students. If the mentor is skilled in the strategy, they can model and teach demonstration lessons for their mentee. If the mentor has knowledge of the strategy, they can suggest professional development activities for the mentee or they may recommend that the mentee observe another teacher who uses the strategy.

Given that each school district uses different strategies and instructional models, a comprehensive discussion of all strategies is beyond the scope of our book. Two reference books that clearly describe instructional strategies are *Strategies for Teaching Students With Learning and Behavior Problems* (5th ed.) by Bos and Vaughn (2002) and *Teaching Children and Adolescents With Special Needs* (4th ed.) by Olson and Platt (2004). The complete citations for these books are in the references section at the end of this chapter.

Diversity of Accommodations. Special education teachers often make curricular accommodations or modifications to help students with disabilities. The main distinction between accommodations and modifications is that accommodations are changes to the way students access instruction and demonstrate performance; whereas modifications are changes to what students are expected to learn (Florida Department of Education, 2003). Teachers can make five types of classroom accommodations:

1. Instructional Methods and Materials

2. Assignments and Assessments

3. Time Demands and Scheduling

4. Learning Environment

5. Use of Special Communications Systems

When special education teachers make accommodations in the area of Instructional Methods and Materials, they alter the way students acquire or use new knowledge. For example if a student has difficulty reading and remembering important information from a textbook, the teacher can provide a chapter outline or summarization. The student can complete the outline while reviewing the chapter. If the student cannot read and comprehend the chapter, he or she could scan the pages into a word processing program that could then be read aloud by a talking word processing program. These types of accommodations provide access to but do not change the content the student is required to learn.

Collaborating With General Educators. The mentor's role in helping the mentee make accommodations is one of offering options. The mentor knows what options are available and what has been successful in the past. They can describe the options open to teachers at their school and help the mentee decide which ones suit the situation. Having an on-site mentor is invaluable to the accommodation process. They provide the new teacher with the history of the school and special education services. White and Mason (2001, pp. 3–4) offer special education mentors the following suggestions when helping mentees with curricular concerns: (a) share copies of your units and student projects, (b) co-plan a lesson built around the general education curriculum standards, (c) show how to make accommodations to a lesson, (d) model successful teaching techniques in their classroom, and (e) show how to order or locate materials. Table 2.4 contains additional ways to make accommodations for instructional methods and materials.

Students typically receive the same types of accommodations for their assignments as they receive on classroom assessments. For instance, if the student is allowed to use a word processor with spelling and grammar check for her written class work, she will need the same accommodation during a written test. Assignment and assessment accommodations may also include the use of calculators, fewer items to complete, and extra time to practice their new skills. These accommodations only change the way students perform; they do not change curricular expectations. In most cases, students receiving assignment and assessment accommodations continue to work toward earning a standard high school diploma (see Table 2.5).

By making accommodations in time demands and scheduling, special education teachers assist students who work or learn at a different pace, those who work better without the pressure of time limits, and those who function better without scheduling demands. Mentors can provide mentees examples of how they make each type of accommodation. For example, Jason Pand offered his mentee the example that, for his students that require additional time to complete assignments, he provides students and parents with a semester calendar containing assignments and due dates so students can plan ahead and start assignments early.

> Another veteran special education teacher, Aaron Dias, had a student with weaknesses in spatial orientation that frequently gets lost moving around the school. Aaron and the IEP team allowed this student to travel to and from classes a few minutes early so that he can use visual landmarks and avoid the chaotic hall environment when classes change.

Time and scheduling accommodations often appeal to new special education teachers because they are easy to implement and require little extra effort (see Table 2.6).

Some students with disabilities may need accommodations in the learning environment to change the physical setting of the classroom, help focus attention, arrange for group work, and assist with individual organization. Other students may need inclusionary, self-contained, or off-campus settings,

Table 2.4   Instructional methods and materials accommodations

Accommodations for Instructional Methods and Materials
Write key points on the board
Give the student a list of important vocabulary
Have the student read the summary and any objectives first
Use peer tutoring instructional model
Provide visual aids or large print
Provide peer note taker
Include a variety of activities during each lesson (e.g., small group, pairs, whole group)
Use hands-on activities coupled with pictures or diagrams
Let the student use sticky notes to mark key points in the textbook
Repeat directions to the student, and have him or her repeat the directions
Provide an outline of the lecture or written material
Allow student to tape-record responses to lessons
Provide an overview of the lesson at the beginning of the class
Use a videotape or DVD that presents the same information
Have students discuss key points orally
Teach through multisensory modes (e.g., visual, auditory, etc.)
Use computer-assisted instruction such as Microsoft PowerPoint.
Accompany oral directions with written directions for child to refer to blackboard or paper
Provide a model to help students; post the model and refer to it often
Provide a book stand to hold materials for easier reading
Teach the student how to make a concept map for note taking
Use examples that students understand and to which they can relate whenever possible
Divide longer lectures or presentations into shorter parts

whereas still others need special furniture, lighting, or acoustics. For the student requiring behavioral accommodations, the IEP team can offer behavior controls, alternative activities for unstructured time, a quiet area where the student may go when necessary, or a positive behavioral support plan. Accommodations made to students' learning environment are often as creative as the IEP team members (see Table 2.7 for suggestions).

Table 2.5   Assignments and assessments accommodations

Assignments and Assessments
Combine verbal directions with charts, words, or pictures
Repeat and simplify instructions for the student
Post a schedule for each day in view of the student
Place a dot on the upper left side of the paper to help the student remember where to start writing
Recognize and give credit for the student's oral participation in class
Minimize lengthy outside reading assignments
Reduce homework assignments
Student should be allowed to use cursive or manuscript writing
Use a prearranged signal (like a clapping pattern) to gain attention before providing directions
Give frequent short quizzes and avoid long tests
Shorten assignments, breaking work into smaller segments
Provide a structured routine in written form
Provide study skills: training and learning strategies
Use a timer to measure the start and stop of work
Give the student a checklist to complete as assignments are finished
Require fewer correct responses to achieve grade (quality versus quantity)
Allow student to tape-record assignments and homework.
Hand out one worksheet at a time
Give the student a choice of assignments
Give partial credit for last assignments
Give the student the rubric used for grading
Reduce the reading level of the assignments
Give extra time to complete tasks
Simplify complex directions
Use color coding to help students identify tasks, meanings, or expectations
Test Taking
Provide the test on audiotape or in large print
Allow open book exams
Let the student use a word processor to write test answers
Give the test orally

Give take-home tests
Highlight important words in the directions
Use more objective items and fewer essay responses
Put the easiest test items first
Allow student to give test answers on tape recorder
Give frequent short quizzes, not long exams
Give partial credit for answers that are partly correct
Allow extra time for exam
Read the test items to the student, when permissible
Avoid placing student under timed conditions
Administer the test individually or in a small group
Let the student retake the test and give credit for improvement
Give frequent breaks during the test

Table 2.6   Accommodations for time and scheduling

Accommodations for Time and Scheduling Demands
Assign a homework buddy
Give assignments ahead of time so the student can start early
Provide peer assistance with organizational skills
Give the student easier tasks first
Allow student to have an extra set of books at home
Develop a reward system for in-school work and homework completion
Give additional time for assignments
Send daily or weekly progress reports home
Provide a clear schedule with frequent checkpoints
Provide each student with a homework assignment notebook

When teachers provide students with accommodations in special communication systems, they provide students with access to expressing themselves and understanding others. These types of accommodations permit students with communication disabilities access to complete participation in classroom activities. Special communications systems benefit students who are hearing impaired, those needing augmentative communication devices, students with limited English proficiency, and nonverbal students. Accommodations include

Table 2.7 Learning environment accommodations

Accommodations for the Learning Environment
Allow the student to sit away from the busiest parts of the classroom
Remove distracting stimuli (e.g., overstimulating bulletin boards, background music, etc.)
Assign specific roles when doing group work
Stand near the student when giving directions or presenting lessons
Use self-checking materials in learning centers
Increase the distance between students' desks
Establish routines for classroom transitions
Seat the student near the teacher
Seat student near a person who is a good role model

SOURCES: Nebraska Department of Education (n.d.); Florida Department of Education (2003).

American Sign Language, finger spelling, lip reading, communication boards, picture symbols, and assistive technology tools.

Mentors should check with their school district or state department of education to determine if local print resources on making accommodations are available to share with mentees. Many resources on making accommodations are located on the Internet; including the informative Web sites: http://www.cpt.fsu.edu/ese/accomm/default.html and the Center for Applied Special Technology (CAST)—http://www.cast.org.

Collaborating With Parents. Parent involvement is a mandatory component of IDEA and some consider it the watchword of the decade. Parent-Teacher Organizations and School Improvement Teams often lead principals' agendas. The special education faculty members play important roles in these parent-school organizations. New special education faculty members need to understand how their school works before they can effectively advocate for their students. The mentor is the best source of information for new teachers regarding the power of parents at their school. The mentor can provide an understanding of what the mission is for the school and how the teachers are involved in the attainment of the mission.

Strong parental support makes any special education teacher's job easier. When parents take an active role in their child's education, the child, teacher, and school usually benefit. Parents can help support their child's education by becoming an advocate for their child and communicating with the teacher on an ongoing basis. Parents help their child by using instructional strategies at home and helping their child with homework. Teachers benefit because they know that if the student experiences a problem, the parents will follow through with intervention or consequences. Last, the school community benefits when

parents volunteer to assist in school activities. Schools with the highest levels of parental support typically earn the highest student test scores on statewide testing. Parental support creates a win-win situation for everyone.

Despite what we know about the benefits of parental involvement, new special education teachers may have little preparation or experience communicating directly with parents. Many preservice teacher preparation programs and alternative certification programs do not structure experiences where students or teachers authentically communicate with parents. New special education teachers may even feel uncomfortable contacting parents to discuss their child. Mentors may need to provide their mentee with ideas, strategies, and techniques to increase and maintain parental involvement.

Usually parents of students in prekindergarten and elementary school are more involved in their child's education than parents of students in middle and secondary school. As a special education teacher, it is beneficial to have parental involvement at every level. Table 2.8 provides suggestions to increase parental communication and conduct effective conferences that mentors can discuss with their mentees.

Collaborating With Paraprofessionals. Paraeducators (paraprofessionals, teachers' aides, or assistants) are a valuable part of special education programs because they support the teacher, students, and the instructional process in general. Many special education teachers work with a paraeducator for part of the school day and need to know how to manage the paraeducator effectively. New special education teachers may need their mentor's support when learning how to work with paraeducators. Paraeducators may have educational background and experience that ranges from attending high school to holding a baccalaureate degree. In addition, some paraeducators have never worked with students and others have worked with students for years. Mentors can help new special education teachers remember that they are the ones held accountable for the progress of students; paraeducators are not.

New special education teachers may begin the school year feeling uneasy about working with another, often older, adult in the classroom.

As a new special education teacher, Heather Hartog felt uneasy about working with her paraeducator because she had 12 years of experience as a paraeducator in special education and already knew all the students. At first, Heather felt at a disadvantage when disciplining the students because the students would "test" her, whereas they did not "test" the paraeducator. Once Heather established herself as a disciplinarian by consistently and fairly applying the classroom rules, she gained confidence in herself and her teaching abilities.

Initially, Heather also wondered if her paraeducator was going to observe her teaching and point out all the mistakes she made as a new special education teacher.

"What if the paraeducator tells other staff members that I am a poor teacher," wondered Heather. "I decided to talk with Mrs. Wooten about

Table 2.8 Communicating with parents

Mentee Guidelines for Communicating With Parents
When possible, personally call or e-mail each parent before school begins to introduce yourself.
During the first week of school, send home a letter explaining your goals for the school year.
Begin positive communication with each parent as early as possible. Building a positive relationship early in the school year will make it easier to deal with a student's problem later.
Keep a parent communication notebook to document each parental contact. Write each student's name at the top of a blank page.
Start each parent communication with something positive about the student. Even a small positive comment builds better parental communication.
Actively listen to the parent's concerns during the conference, and validate that his or her concerns are important. Consider that the parent knows the child best.
When in doubt about the special education services available to a student, let the parent know that you are aware of their request and that you will find out the answer as soon as possible.
Always keep a professional demeanor during conferences, and keep in mind that everyone is working for the student's benefit.
When communicating with parents that do not speak English as their first language, arrange for a translator to translate your spoken or written communication.
Keep in mind the variations of each culture and be sensitive to cultural differences such as using formal greetings rather than the parent's first name.
When preplanning for a parent conference, warmly greet the parent and maintain eye contact when speaking to the parent.
During a parent-teacher conference, keep professional jargon and the use of acronyms to a minimum. Many parents are not familiar with common acronyms such as *IEP* or *LD*.
Begin the conference by discussing the student's strengths, followed by an update on any previous problems.
Explain the purpose for today's conference, and outline any student problems and what you think may be causing the problems.
Gather parent insight on the student's current academic or social functioning. Ask parents if there might be issues outside of school that are affecting the student's performance.
Discuss strategies for addressing the student's problem.
Explain the actions you will take to help the student, and ask the parent if they are willing to take action at home to help.
Set a communication method (e.g., notes home, phone calls, e-mail), and schedule an appointment to meet again to review the student's progress.
End the conference on a positive note.

Table 2.9   Guidelines for working with paraeducators

Working With Paraeducators
The special education teacher is the primary decision-maker in the classroom.
Use diplomacy when making final decisions, and use delicacy in how you use your authority.
Discuss clearly defined roles and responsibilities.
Discuss classroom operating procedures (e.g., who will grade students' academic work or monitor them during recess).
Do not argue with your paraprofessional. If you have attempted to collaboratively solve problems without success, bring the problems to a higher authority.
Discuss how to handle students that try to play you against each other.
Discuss maintaining behavior point sheets.
Discuss assisting students that arrive and leave on the school bus.
Discuss who will contact parents.
Discuss how to provide assistance to students individually or in groups.
Discuss how to ensure confidentiality.
Discuss how to deal with disagreements productively.
Discuss how to monitor student behavior.

the role she would play in my classroom. She told me what the teacher did last year and I used my mentor's advice to help her see her role this year."

Heather and her paraeducator maintained a positive relationship by keeping open lines of communication throughout the school year. Mentors can offer their mentee the guidelines for working with paraeducators located in Table 2.9.

Compounding of Teacher Roles. Special education teachers are often required to assume different roles within the educational system. Many special education teachers provide different types of support to their special education students within the course of a single day. A special education teacher may start the day by coteaching in an inclusive classroom, move to a resource classroom for one or two class periods, and end the day providing consultation to general education teachers. In addition, the special education teacher is responsible for communicating with parents, completing paperwork, ensuring legal compliance, and collaborating with other professionals. This multiplicity of roles is often overwhelming to a new special education teacher who enters the field thinking she will always teach in a self-contained setting.

If the new special education teacher is not skilled at multitasking, then the novice will need help in prioritizing their day. One clue for the mentor is to determine the type of placement the mentee had in their student teaching. If the mentee completed student teaching in a self-contained class, they may need more direction in meeting the demands of a resource or multisetting special education classroom.

Special education mentors can provide emotional support to mentees as they adjust to the complex responsibilities of their position. Mentors can help to focus the mentee on the most critical issues to address first. Many times the mentee does not understand the big picture of their job because they are faced with many smaller tasks and issues that obscure their view. Melissa Conway explained her views:

> When I began teaching I felt pulled in every direction so that I was giving up my lunch and planning time so students' schedules would work out, I could attend committee meetings, co-plan with the inclusion teacher, and direct my paraprofessional. I was extremely stressed out.

Fortunately, Melissa's mentor understood her situation and helped her regain her planning time by meeting with the guidance counselor to correct students' schedules. This helped Melissa focus on establishing a good relationship with her paraeducator and the inclusion teachers she worked with on a daily basis. Without her mentor's support and knowledge of who was authorized to make schedule changes, Melissa would have burned out of teaching quickly. Mentors can consider their responses to the questions in Table 2.10 to help mentees deal with occupational complexities.

Cultural Diversity Issues. The IEP team must attend to the cultural and language differences of all students. Ortiz (1997, pp. 331–332) makes three recommendations when considering cultural differences: (1) Language models of the home may be functional for the home setting but not of the same language status as needed to succeed in the academic or school setting. (2) Students with low skills in both language and academics may not have the beginning language base needed to add on daily academic information. Academic difficulties are compounded even more with the structure of classroom expectations. For example, academic information changes hourly with each subject and weekly for subject units. (3) Students with a lack of opportunity to learn in relation to their cultural background, education, and poverty will lack learning experiences, demonstrate low vocabulary, content, ideas, and overall descriptive language difficulties. Cummins (1984) estimated that, on average, students with limited English proficiency (LEP) acquire conversational skills in one to two years but need five to seven years to achieve academic language proficiency.

Special education teachers should consider students' cultural and linguistic heritage in all aspects of instruction. With today's student population becoming more culturally and linguistically diverse and the teaching profession remaining predominantly white, special education teachers should develop cultural competence. Miller (2002) defines cultural competence as the teacher's "Ability to respond to all students in ways that acknowledge and respect their cultural and linguistic diversity" (p. 314). New special education teachers may be less aware of the needs of diverse students than veteran

Table 2.10   Mentee's frequently asked questions

Common Questions of Mentees	Potential Responses
1. How do I make time to co-plan with each inclusion teacher?	
2. Should I grade every student assignment?	
3. How do I order supplies?	
4. How do I prepare for a field trip or community outing?	
5. What can I do to help this student read, when nothing I do seems to work?	
6. How do I handle disruptive students?	
7. How do I determine what the general education teacher is teaching?	
8. What are the procedures for dispensing medication to students?	
9. Who plans for my paraprofessional's day?	
10. What if my paraprofessional and I don't get along?	
11. Other:	

special education teachers. Mentors can help mentees by offering curricular materials that integrate multiculturalism into the content. Although few instructional practices exist for specific cultural differences, many teaching methods such as cooperative learning, mnemonic devices, active learning materials, and multisensory teaching are used successfully with diverse groups of students. Table 2.11 contains suggestions for teaching culturally diverse students.

SPECIAL EDUCATION PROCESSES

Attending and conducting IEP meetings are common events for special education teachers. Most school districts have a unique IEP format although all IEPs are required to have specific components. Mentors can assist mentees by making sure each IEP they write contains the required components and meets the school district's standard for accountability. Each IEP must contain the following:

- Present level of educational performance

- Measurable annual goals, including benchmarks or short-term objectives

- Special education and related services

Table 2.11   Teaching suggestions for culturally diverse students

African-American Students

- Use cooperative learning instructional strategies.
- Use mnemonic activities (e.g., acronyms, pictures as memory aids).
- Use interactive activities (e.g., computer-assisted instruction; peer tutoring, group work, use manipulative devices).
- Include movement-for-learning activities (e.g., theatrics or role-playing, rhythmics or beating, clapping).

Asian- and Pacific-American Students

- Secure and maintain positive relationships with parents.
- Provide bilingual education.
- Provide a culturally affirming learning environment.
- Provide programs to help students and parents understand and cope with anxiety related to high-achievement expectations and pressure.
- Provide positive role models that have struck a balance among diverse ethnic, religious, peer, family, neighborhood, and school expectations.
- Select and use literature with positive Asian role models.
- Provide opportunities for students to work collaboratively.

Mexican-American Students

- Emphasize functional communication between teacher and students and among students themselves.
- Conduct many comprehension checks to ensure students understand assignments.
- Emphasize student collaboration on small-group projects organized around learning centers.
- Limit worksheet exercises.
- Use thematic units to organize basic skill and content instruction.
- Provide many opportunities for students to assist one another with learning activities.
- Allow students to use either English or Spanish.

Native American Students

- Integrate Native American cultural values into the curriculum.
- Avoid discrediting Native Americans when teaching American history.
- De-emphasize competition.
- Reduce lecturing.
- Use motor, visual, tactile, or auditory games and activities.
- Allow longer pauses after questioning.
- Use peer learning.

Hispanic Students

- Establish links to the community.
- Develop strong parent involvement in schools.
- Maintain high expectations for all students.
- Provide Hispanic role models.
- Provide bilingual and bicultural programs.
- Acknowledge and affirm Hispanic diversity and shared values.
- Promote students' use of native and second language.

SOURCE: From Susan Peterson Miller, *Validated Practices for Teaching Students With Diverse Needs and Abilities.* Published by Allyn and Bacon, Boston, MA. Copyright © 2002 by Pearson Education. Reprinted by permission of the publisher.

- Explanation of nonparticipation in general education curriculum when necessary

- Participation in statewide or district-wide assessments or, if determined by the IEP Team, a statement of alternate assessment

- Dates, frequency, location, and duration of services

- Student progress (measuring and reporting)

- Transition services

- Transfer of rights (if applicable)

- Extended school year

The IEP is the document that assures the student is receiving a free, appropriate public education. Each IEP is uniquely developed to meet the needs of a child with a disability. The IEP is a working document that provides staff with guidance for day-to-day instruction. Special education teachers should keep a copy of the students' IEP in their classroom to refer to as needed. The IEP is a document that must meet legal mandates. Anytime the IEP team is considering the development, revision, or review of a student's IEP, the team must have a discussion of the student's strengths, parental concerns, evaluation results, special factors behavior, limited English proficiency, Braille, communication needs, and assistive technology. Special education teachers can use the IEP checklist in Table 2.12 when preparing for and conducting IEP meetings.

Effective Instruction. Teaching is a complex field influenced by many variables. New special education teachers are typically in a survival mode when school begins and then start to gradually gain confidence and competence. As mentors observe their mentees and provide suggestions for improving their teaching, they should focus on giving feedback about the teaching behaviors that are associated with increased student achievement. Christenson, Ysseldyke, and Thurlow (1989) report that effective special education teachers should consider ten essential factors when teaching students with mild disabilities. These factors include the degree to which:

1. Classroom management is effective and efficient. Teachers need effective classroom management to increase the amount of time available for instruction. Efficiency is an important part of time management to ensure that classroom management is proactive and eliminates behaviors that waste time.

2. There is a sense of "positiveness" in the school environment. Student achievement is higher if the classroom climate is orderly, cooperative learning is used, and there is strong administrative leadership.

3. There is an appropriate instructional match. Special education teachers should identify student weaknesses and design motivating and interesting instructional activities to strengthen these areas.

Table 2.12   Checklist of IEP duties

Preparing and Conducting IEP Meetings
Follow school district procedures for notifying parents (and the student, when appropriate) about the IEP meeting, and schedule a mutually agreeable date and time.
Decide which general education teacher(s) should attend, and gather information from other general education teachers.
Two to four weeks before the IEP is written, administer formal and informal tests. Score and analyze student performance.
Gather student work samples and performance data in a folder or binder.
Generate draft statements for the student's current level of performance.
Prepare a draft of the student's possible annual goals and short-term objectives.
If the student is 14 years old or older, interview the student to gather data for the transition IEP.
If the student will participate in the IEP meeting, brief him or her about the format and appropriate times to contribute. Teach the student how to lead the IEP meeting using a program such as the Self-Directed IEP (Martin, Marshall, Maxon, & Jerman, 1998).
At the meeting, arrive organized and ready to present your information when requested. Be concise and stay on topic.
Encourage parent comments.
Discuss postconference support that you will continue to provide the student.
Complete the IEP to the best of your ability, and obtain all required signatures.
Give the parents a copy of the IEP, and make a copy to keep in your classroom.

4. Teaching goals and teacher expectations for student performance and success are stated clearly and are understood by the student. The teaching goals are considered the blueprint for classroom instruction and activities. Special education teachers must clearly state goals and make sure students understand the goal and the accompanying activity's importance.

5. Lessons are presented clearly and follow specific instructional procedures. Lessons should comprise the following: begin with a review, a rationale for what is to be learned, demonstration procedures and explanation of the content, guided practice, independent practice, and a summarization.

6. Instructional support is provided for the individual student. Special education teachers should be skilled in adjusting or adapting instruction so that a high success rate is maintained. Students should be taught to monitor their own thinking by using teacher "think alouds."

7. Sufficient time is allocated to academics and instructional time is used efficiently. Special education teachers should ensure that students have sufficient academic engaged time to practice new academic skills.

8. The student's opportunity to respond is high. According to Christensen and colleagues, students actively engaged in making academic responses such as writing or reading aloud make greater academic gains.

9. The teacher actively monitors student progress and understanding. When teachers monitor instruction it results in an appropriate match between instruction and student need.

10. Student performance is evaluated appropriately and frequently. When student evaluation occurs often and in alignment with the curriculum, teachers gain information to modify instructions and make instructional decisions.

Reflective Practices. The new special education teacher should reflect on each instructional lesson taught. Self-reflection is a form of self-assessment because it allows us to examine our own performance and think about areas that were effective and areas that need to be strengthened. Becoming good at self-reflection is a skill that takes time and practice to develop. Mentors can help new special education teachers by talking through a think-aloud procedure after teaching a lesson. By sharing your thoughts aloud, the mentee gains insight into how to use reflective thinking as an ongoing process to promote positive changes. Gradually change the role so the mentee begins to use a think aloud after a lesson the mentor observes.

New special education teachers can use reflective thinking in all areas related to the school day but should begin by reflecting on their performance during the instructional planning process of preplanning, interactive planning, and postplanning. Special education teachers preplan for a lesson when they consider the goal of the lesson, available curriculum materials, needs of the student, classroom environment, and their own interest in the topic being taught. Interactive planning is the type of planning a teacher does while teaching the lesson. She may notice that a student does not understand her explanation, so she makes up another example that the student can relate to and understand. Postplanning occurs after the lesson is taught and the teacher considers issues such as whether or not the lesson's goal was accomplished, how students interacted together, and what she would do differently the next time. The new special education teacher can pinpoint strengths and weaknesses by reflecting on each component of the planning process individually (see Table 2.13). If there is one area of weakness, the mentor can help provide resources and make suggestions to strengthen that area.

Assessment of Student Progress. Special education is a field that relies upon ongoing assessment of students in order to document their progress and growth. Special education teachers and other professionals frequently use norm-referenced measures to document the effectiveness of intervention, document an existing disability, and assist in determining eligibility for special

Table 2.13   Reflective planning guide

Planning Stage	Reflective Thoughts: Positives	Reflective Thoughts: Needs and Actions
Preplanning		
Interactive Planning		
Postplanning		

education services. Norm-referenced assessment measures allow teachers to compare the performance of a student in a class to a sample of same age or grade students. Most norm-referenced assessment measures allow teachers to report students' scores as standard scores, percentiles, and age or grade equivalents.

Scores reported as percentile ranks indicate the student's position in relation to the standardization sample of students. For example, a percentile rank of 89 indicates the student scored at or above 89% of other students the same age. Standard scores are raw scores that have been changed to have an average and a standard deviation that express how far a student's score is from average. A student's standard score of 116 means he scored one standard deviation above average, or in the high-average range. Grade equivalents refer to the level of test performance of an average student at that grade. It does not mean that the student can perform curricular tasks for that grade level at his or her school. All three types of scores are used on the IEP to report the student's performance.

Each student's IEP contains information on how his or her performance is assessed and documented. Students with disabilities typically participate in statewide assessments, annual norm-referenced assessments, and curriculum-based assessments. In addition, many research-based instructional techniques (such as DIBELS and SIM) include assessments that teachers use to document their students' progress.

New special education teachers should know the most frequently used assessment measures in special education or the frequently used assessment measures within their school district. New special education teachers that graduated from university teacher preparation programs completed at least one course on measures of student assessment. New special education teachers who complete alternative certification routes to special education may or may not have experience with assessment instruments. These mentees may not know that many special education assessment instruments, such as the Woodcock-Johnson Tests of Achievement, have standardized administration procedures. Mentees may rely upon their mentor to answer questions such as, "Which assessments require following a prescribed procedure and which ones do not require specific wording? Which tests have basals and ceilings that must be established?" Without knowledge of assessment instruments, the mentee may receive invalid or inaccurate test results. The special education mentor can use the new Mentee Needs Checklist (p. 6) or informal interview to find out their mentee's knowledge of student assessment. Using this knowledge, the mentor can either provide instruction on how to administer a particular instrument or direct the mentee to a professional development opportunity.

A plethora of norm-referenced assessment measures are available and used in special education. Some of the most frequently used measures are described in Resource C. It is best that the mentor and mentee develop a list of tests that are suitable for their school rather than purchasing tests at random from any listing of assessments.

Behavior Management. Classroom management solutions appear at the top of every new teacher's wish list. It is the one area that can cause a teacher to rethink his or her career choice. Most teacher preparation programs include classroom management courses; however, it seems it is never enough to help a new teacher get started smoothly. Although many authors on the topic address what to do the first week of school, Kyle and Rogien (2004) describe the beginning of the year in terms of preventative, supportive, and corrective discipline choices.

Preventative discipline involves everything you do before you teach to make teaching go smoothly. This includes room layout, scheduling centers or computer time, classroom rules and procedures, and grading and evaluation procedures. In Resource C you will find a listing of classroom management references to help new teachers with preventative discipline. Of particular interest would be Sprick, Garrison, and Howard's book *CHAMPs: Proactive and Positive Approach to Classroom Management* (1998, Module 2).

Supportive discipline refers to what teachers do while teaching to manage behavior. This form of discipline is stylistic and subtle in nature. Experienced teachers do it unconsciously. They remind students of the rules for walking to and from the cafeteria before they even line up. That's supportive discipline. New teachers need time and experience to effectively incorporate this element of discipline into their daily routines. Mentor teachers can help by modeling for the mentee how and when they support their own discipline plans. Discipline in action is enhanced by the teacher's efforts to connect with students. In general, students want to know their teacher cares about them as individuals. Building rapport with students is a very important part of managing the class.

The last type of discipline choices identified by Kyle and Rogien (2004) are the corrective choices. These are the discipline actions a teacher takes in the midst of a management situation. Effective outcomes here rely on the teacher's ability to design, teach, and reinforce a management plan within their class. Regardless of whether it's a token economy, level system model, or cost response model, the key is consistent attention to the desired behaviors.

The mentor is most helpful to the mentee when acting as a sounding board, allowing the mentee to talk about how they are handling discipline issues. By listening and asking thought-provoking questions that get at why a decision was made, the mentor can help the mentee clarify their beliefs about discipline and about how they want their class to run. The mentor can use the questions in Table 2.14 to help with the discipline choice discussion.

Table 2.14 Things to consider when setting up classroom rules

Developing a classroom climate you can live with

Which one sounds most like you?

Noise level	• I should be able to hear a pin drop • Some whispering is OK, but I don't want to hear students talking • Kids need to talk when they work together—they still need to hear me
Movement	• Everyone in their seats • Respect each other's space • Hands up to ask permission to leave your seat • Move around only as appropriate • Students can move around when they work in groups
Getting help	• Students should raise their hands to ask for help • You can ask for help from any adult in the room • Ask your neighbor first, and then ask the teacher
Responsibility	• If you're late, see me later to get work • Use your class buddy to get extra copies to the work missed • Your work is located in a work folder in case you miss it

The mentor and mentee should think about how true these statements are for the mentee. The choices they make can help formulate the class rules and procedures. For example, a teacher who wants to hear a pin drop in his or her classroom will not be comfortable with cooperative learning groups. They should not try this routine in their classroom, as it will make them unhappy and will cause problems with management. The mentor has to assure the mentee that there are other ways to teach besides cooperative learning groups. The underlying message is that the management choices you make are directly related to the system of discipline you feel most at ease with. The novice teacher may not realize that having students lose their recess privileges means that the teacher who has to monitor the detention is also losing some privileges. In some teachers' minds that may not be fair. Matching the teacher beliefs to practices is key to making the classroom rules and procedures work. Table 2.15 offers general classroom management suggestions for mentors working with new special education teachers.

Curriculum Adaptation. Motivating students with special needs can produce anxiety for teachers because many times these students are hesitant to take risks for fear of failing (Jonson, 2002). In many instances, by the time students enter the fifth grade or higher, they may have already experienced failure for two or more years. Repeated failure in any activity results in a lack of desire or motivation in the student to participate in that activity. Think about your own experiences with repeated failure in an activity. I am terrible at golf. My repeated failures playing golf included friends teasing me, embarrassment

Table 2.15   Classroom management support ideas for mentors

Classroom Management Concerns: Ideas for Mentors
Help the mentee develop classroom rules and consequences.
Help arrange the physical layout of the classroom.
Share your classroom schedule, or develop one together.
Discuss how students should enter and exit the classroom.
Share suggestions for grouping students during instruction.
Discuss how and when students should move throughout the classroom.
Help the mentee design a record-keeping system.
Provide the mentee with suggestions for transition or downtime.
Other:
Other:

when playing around other, more skilled golfers, and a lot of frustration. Consider that I'm an adult and can handle the teasing and feelings of frustration. What if I was then told that during almost every activity of my day I have to use golfing techniques? I would feel discouraged and hopeless. The student with the learning disability feels the same way. Consider the student with a specific learning disability in reading who receives intensive reading instruction during the school day, works with a reading tutor after school, and works with one or both parents on reading in the evening and on weekends. This student practically spends all day trying to perform an activity that he or she does not particularly like and that is extremely hard. Strikingly, teachers and parents then wonder why the student is not motivated to read. Perhaps when the student experiences success in reading the motivation to read will increase.

Special education teachers can help motivate their students by:

- Designing instructional activities so the student is successful
- Providing materials of high interest
- Designing instructional activities that use the student's strengths to counter weaknesses
- Incorporating hands-on and experiential activities into instruction
- Having fun
- Maintaining high but realistic expectations for success
- Using cooperative learning activities
- Implementing instructional accommodations for difficult tasks
- Providing extra time to complete tasks
- Giving outlines, copies of notes, and other aids to help with learning

Table 2.16   Student interest inventory

Name: _____   Date: _____

Interest Inventory

Directions: Place a check mark ☑ next to the 10 things you enjoy most.

	Collecting cards		Reading
	Playing baseball		Bike riding
	Playing basketball		Playing with friends
	Playing soccer		Skateboarding
	Playing lacrosse		Rollerblading
	Playing hockey		Taking care of animals
	Playing softball		Fishing
	Bowling		Swimming
	Gymnastics		Working on the computer
	Dancing		Playing video games
	Going to the park		Playing a musical instrument
	Going to the movies		Drawing
	Skiing		Painting
	Hiking		Arts and crafts
	Playing board games		Watching TV
	Cooking: making and eating food		Acting or drama
	Car racing		Listening to music
	Horseback riding		Dinosaurs
	Other:		Other:

New special education teachers can also use an interest inventory with students to find out their specific areas of interest. Teachers can use students' interests to plan instructional and reinforcement activities. If the student with a reading learning disability has a keen interest in planets, the teacher may locate high-interest, low-difficulty books on planets for the student to use during free time and at home. Table 2.16 contains a reproducible interest inventory for students.

PROFESSIONAL ISSUES

Socialization. Although most people do not realize it before becoming a teacher, teaching can be an isolating profession. Even though a teacher is with students all day, there may be few opportunities for adult interaction. Once teachers enter their own classroom, they have entered their own domain and rarely have the opportunity to observe others teaching or seek answers when questions arise. Without viewing demonstration lessons from their mentor or the support from an administrator who provides release time for the mentee to go observe others, the mentee is often isolated in the classroom. This loneliness can become an awful feeling of isolation, one that most teachers experience at some point in their career (Jonson, 2002; Whitaker, 2001).

To make the mentee's first year less isolating, the school administrator can arrange the same planning time for the mentor and mentee. A common planning time allows the mentor and mentee to discuss questions, issues, and teaching ideas. If the mentor and mentee are in different schools, the administrator can provide release time for a support meeting. Release time to observe other teachers as well as time to meet with mentors is viewed as critical by beginning special education teachers (White & Mason, 2001).

Mentors can help mentees think broadly about their contributions to each student, the school, the community, and the profession of special education.

New special education teachers often remain in the survival mode for the first months of school. During this time mentees do not consider the profession as a whole, but rather on their experiences as new special education teachers. As the mentee grows more confident with his position, there is a gradual shift from self-centeredness to a student-oriented approach, followed by reflection on contributing to greater entities such as the school and the profession. In Table 2.17 below, The National Clearinghouse for Professions in Special Education (1998) offers ten suggestions for helping new special education teachers grow and contribute professionally.

Job Satisfaction. New special education teachers' job satisfaction influences the incidence of teacher burnout. It's important to remember that all special education teachers experience times when they feel discouraged or unenthusiastic about their job. Many factors, such as paperwork, lack of administrative support, student behavior, isolation, and others, contribute to special education teachers leaving the teaching profession at a faster rate than general education teachers (Griffin, Winn, Otis-Wilborn, & Kilgore, 2003). Mentors are a key part of the mentee's support system and effective mentoring has a powerful effect on the mentee's job satisfaction. Along with administrator support and having adequate teaching materials, mentor support is ranked high among new special education teachers.

Westling and Koorland (1988) offer special education teachers the following suggestions to reduce stress and avoid burnout:

- Make time for yourself and nurture your personal needs

- Maintain a positive outlook during stressful situations

Table 2.17   Professional development ideas

Professional Development Ideas
Get involved in professional development opportunities offered by the school district.
Facilitate student responsibility for accepting leadership from alternate staff so that you have the opportunity to leave the classroom when necessary.
Be an advocate for yourself and your profession.
Read literature and the latest research. Be informed.
Don't compromise the quality of your work by overextending yourself.
Learn to evaluate the appropriateness of your employment site.
Engage in conversation with general education professionals to learn about what they think they need to know.
Volunteer to be a conduit to educate other school personnel regarding special education issues.
Ensure you are communicating with external constituents, including parents and community resource representatives.
Capitalize on opportunities for positive visibility within and outside of your school.

- Keep healthy by eating right and exercising

- Change your environment by rearranging your classroom

- Take weekend vacations

- Maintain outside interests and hobbies unrelated to teaching

- Enlist the help of parents and volunteers to help with daily tasks such as copying and grading of papers

Shaw, Bensky, and Dixon (1981) offer teachers classic stress management tips in the areas of organization, change, and attitude.

Organize Your Time and Activities

- **Set realistic and flexible professional goals and objectives.** Don't set expectations that will be impossible to meet.

- **Establish priorities** to deal with needs in the order of importance.

- **Leave your work at school.** Bringing work home after school can cause problems in that it often interferes with personal and family life. One way to break that cycle is to avoid bringing work home.

- **Pace yourself.** Approaches to help avoid wasting time and prevent procrastination include setting realistic timelines, getting high priority work done early in the day and including time for you each day. Do *not* try to do everything at once.

- **Use available human resources.** Use the available human resources to their maximum potential. Take the extra time necessary to train an aide or secretary to handle more responsibilities independently.

- **Organize your classroom.** Improved classroom organization can save time and increase professional productivity.

Be Open to Change, Innovation, and New Opportunities

- **Change your environment.**

- **Keep yourself motivated.** Seeking out new experiences can be one way to maintain professional interest and prevent stagnation. A special educator can try new instructional techniques, implement alternative programs, or develop new materials.

- **Consider career options.** There are many alternative career avenues that special educators and special services personnel should consider for diversifying their experience or stimulating interest. Career options include placement team coordinator, consultant, and inservice coordinator.

- **Seek out personal learning experiences.** Professional and personal growth requires that we keep learning. Programs that provide new skills needed on the job or that broaden your base of knowledge are ideal.

Be Positive About Yourself and Your Profession

- **Allow a "moment of glory"** to accept and acknowledge positive feedback.

- **Look for the "silver lining."** It is often helpful to seek out the "silver lining" in an otherwise dismal situation.

- **Become directly involved.** In many cases, working directly to deal with the issues that cause problems can be both therapeutic and productive.

- **Remember the children you serve.** Remember why you have chosen to be a special education teacher. Focus on the personal, professional, and philosophical reasons you became a teacher.

Additional stress-reducing activities reported by Griffin et al. (2003) in their special education teacher induction report included participating in stress management workshops, peer collaboration training, and using reflection journals. By collectively working with a mentor and using different supports and stress management techniques, new special education teachers can develop a long-lasting career in special education.

Professional Development. Ongoing professional development is an important part of a successful career in special education. Whether new special education teachers graduate from college or complete an alternate certification program, their knowledge of the field of special education is just beginning. As we know, learning is a lifelong process, and college courses and applied experiences provide the knowledge base that will continue to grow throughout our careers. Once we begin teaching our own class of students, our prior knowledge is strengthened with our experiences and we learn what really works and things that do not work. We generate new questions about teaching techniques and student characteristics that motivate us to find answers. As a new special education teacher, questions that I had were, "Why was a student promoted to the eighth grade who still reads on a primer level?" "Why does a student push his books on the floor and call me names when I give him work that is at his independent level?" Questions like these prompted me to continue my professional development by participating in additional workshops, attending professional conferences, and taking college courses. Through these professional development activities, my questions were answered.

Continuing professional development is also important as new educational research emerges and new techniques are developed to help students with disabilities and their teachers. A recent issue of *CEC Today* (2003), the membership newsletter for the Council for Exceptional Children, contained an article on the latest brain imaging research using MRIs to determine differences in the brains of students with and without learning disabilities. The article further described how brain-based research is helping teachers of students with disabilities. Membership in professional organizations can help alert teachers to new research and accompanying professional development opportunities. In addition, each school district's exceptional student education department sponsors numerous workshops and professional development activities throughout the school year for special education teachers.

Professional development is important for new special education teachers to stay current with changes in federal and state laws. As we write this book, the Individuals with Disabilities Education Act is being reauthorized. Many questions remain about the components required in the individual education plan, student discipline, and the criteria used for identification of students with learning disabilities. Active professional development gives new special education teachers access to the most current information that influences their teaching conditions. By being actively involved in professional development and organizations, new special education teachers can lobby for the values they believe are most important. Special education teachers can join professional organizations such as the Council for Exceptional Children. A listing of professional organizations in special education is available in Resource C.

An additional advantage of being a member of a professional organization is that you receive the organization's publications (such as journals, magazines, and newsletters). Many of these resources, such as *Teaching Exceptional Children,* are aimed at practicing special education teachers and contain validated practices that are feasible to implement. Other publications contain

the latest research in special education. All of these resources provide timely information that can benefit special education mentors and mentees. A list of professional publications for special education teachers can be found in Resource C.

WHAT IF?

I teach my students using a research-validated instructional practice that I know improves their paragraph writing skills. The students in my mentee's classroom need to improve their writing but she only wants them to free write and will not consider using the strategy I recommend. What should I do?

As a mentor you cannot force the mentee to use the strategy, regardless of its effectiveness. The school administrator may require the teacher to use the strategy. We suggest that you try several approaches.

1. Arrange for the mentee to observe you teaching the strategy.

2. Assist the mentee in preparing any materials or engineering the classroom before using the strategy.

3. Offer to teach the strategy to his or her class the first time the strategy is introduced.

4. Schedule time to periodically observe each other teaching the strategy.

5. Determine whether any district-level supports are available to help the mentee.

REFERENCES

Bos, C. S., & Vaughn, S. (2002). *Strategies for teaching students with learning and behavior problems* (5th ed.). Boston: Allyn & Bacon.

Bova, B. M., & Phillips, R. E. (1981). *The mentor relationship: A study of mentors and protégés in business and academia.* (Report No. CE 030362). New Mexico. (ERIC Document Reproduction Service No. ED 208233)

Carnine, D. (1994). The BIG accommodations program. *Educational Leadership, 51*(6), 87–88.

CEC Today. (2003). Brain research: Brain research sheds new light on student learning, teaching strategies, and disabilities. Retrieved November 1, 2003, from http://www.cec.sped.org/bk/cectoday/?module=displaystory&story_id=750&format=html

Christenson, S. L., Ysseldyke, J. E., & Thurlow, M. L. (1989). Critical instructional factors for students with mild handicaps: An integrative review. *Remedial and Special Education, 10*(5), 21–31.

Council for Exceptional Children. (2003). *What every special educator must know: The international standards for the preparation and certification of special education teachers* (5th ed.). Reston, VA: Author.

Cummins, J. (1984). *Bilingualism and special education: Issues in assessment and pedagogy.* San Diego, CA: College-Hill.

Engelmann, S., Becker, W. C., Carnine, D., & Gersten, R. (1988). The direct instruction follow through model: Design and outcomes. *Education and Treatment of Children, 11*(4), 303–317.

Florida Department of Education. (2003). *Accommodations: Assisting students with disabilities (a guide for educators)*. Tallahassee, FL: Author.

Griffin, C. C., Winn, J. A., Otis-Wilborn, A., & Kilgore, K. L. (2003). *New teacher induction in special education*. Retrieved August 6, 2003, from http://www.coe.ufl.edu/coppse/

Jonson, K. F. (2002). *Being an effective mentor: How to help beginning teachers succeed*. Thousand Oaks, CA: Corwin Press.

Kyle, P. B., & Rogien, L. R. (2004). *Opportunities and options in classroom management*. New York: Pearson Educational.

Martin, J. E., Marshall, L. H., Maxon, L., & Jerman, P. (1998). *The self-directed IEP kit*. Longmont, CO: Sopris West.

Meese, R. L. (2001). *Teaching learners with mild disabilities: Integrating research and practice* (2nd ed.). Belmont, CA: Wadsworth/Thompson Learning.

Miller, S. P. (2002). *Validated practices for teaching students with diverse needs and abilities*. Boston: Allyn & Bacon.

National Clearinghouse for Professionals in Special Education. (1998). *Retention of special education professionals: A practical guide of strategies and activities for educators and administrators*. Reston, VA: Council for Exceptional Children.

Nebraska Department of Education. (n.d.). *Example of an instructional accommodations format*. Retrieved July 29, 2004, from http://www.nde.state.ne.us/SPED/iepproj/appc/eacc.html

Olson, J. L., & Platt, J. C. (2004). *Teaching children and adolescents with special needs* (4th ed). Upper Saddle River, NJ: Pearson Merrill Prentice Hall.

Ortiz, A. A. (1997). Learning disabilities occurring concomitantly with linguistic differences. *Journal of Learning Disabilities 30*, 321–332.

Shaw, S. F., Bensky, J. M., & Dixon, B. (1981). *Stress and burnout: A primer for special education and special services personnel*. Reston, VA: Council for Exceptional Children.

Sprick, R., Garrison, M., & Howard, L. M. (1998). *CHAMPs: A proactive and positive approach to classroom management for grades K–9*. Longmont, CO: Sopris West.

Westling, D. L., & Koorland, M. A. (1988). *The special educator's handbook*. Boston: Allyn & Bacon.

White, W. A. T. (1988). A meta-analysis of the effects of direct instruction in special education. *Education and Treatment of Children, 22*(5), 259–272.

White, M., & Mason, C. (2001). The mentoring induction project: What new teachers need from mentors. *Teaching Exceptional Children, 33*(6), 81.

Whitaker, S. D. (2001). Supporting beginning special education teachers. *Focus on Exceptional Children, 34*(4), 1–18.

Designing Mentoring Programs 3

VIGNETTE

We knew that a mentoring program specifically designed for the new special education teachers was needed in our district but initially we were concerned because of our district's small size. We are considered a rural school district and we are limited by resources and funding as to the support and services we can provide. Plus, there is a general new teacher induction program that is a requirement for all teachers, so we did not want to reinvent the wheel. At the same time, special education teachers have some unique issues of their own that require support.

With four elementary schools, two middle schools, and one high school, we do not have that many special education teachers who can serve as mentors. In addition to not having a lot of special education mentor teachers in our district, we often only have one or two special education teachers at a school. This makes it difficult to pair a new special education teacher with a mentor that is teaching the same types of students. Often a new special education teacher is mentored by a general education teacher from that school or a special education teacher from another school. Do we like this? In the ideal world we would not choose this arrangement but it was the best we could do given our resources.

Currently we are partnering with our state's Comprehensive System of Personnel Development to implement an induction program for special education teachers. Is it easy to accomplish? No, but we are making excellent progress and have a pilot program in existence. Informal feedback from the mentors and mentees is positive. We headed in the right direction! One of my teachers summed it up by saying, "I think this is an excellent program which should be expanded. It allows experienced ESE teachers to share their knowledge in a nonthreatening way and sets up the new or out-of-field teacher for success."

—Special Education Director

CRITICAL ELEMENTS FOR DESIGNING EFFECTIVE MENTORING PROGRAMS

A properly designed mentoring program is a powerful and cost-effective tool for supporting and retaining new special education teachers. Special education teachers who have the support of mentor teachers are more likely to remain in the profession (Council for Exceptional Children, 2000). According to the Oregon Special Education Recruitment and Retention Project (2002), districts which implemented strong teacher support systems achieved a five-year teacher retention rate of 70%–80%. Lloyd, Wood, and Moreno (2000) identified that a training program for special education mentors should consist of the following critical elements: (a) the role of the mentor teacher; (b) tactics for working with adult peers; (c) ways to establish rapport and trust with the new teacher; and (d) strategies to provide feedback that is both positive and constructive. Additional critical elements to embed in a mentoring program include: mentor incentives, a proper mentor-mentee match, ongoing and adequate support for special education issues, system information related to special education, and others.

But perhaps one of the most important elements for a successful mentoring program is a visible commitment from the special education director, district staff, school-based teachers, and all special education personnel involved—a commitment that quality new teacher induction and mentoring are a key part of the department's philosophy. The risk of failure is minimized when all key stakeholders have the same core philosophical agreement and an aligned vision to create a model new teacher support program. A successful special education mentoring program is not built by one person alone, but by a team of dedicated individuals working together to customize the activities and resources presented in this book to the unique needs of each school district's special education department. Furthermore, as elaborated in this chapter, the special education mentoring program is a fluid program that evolves from ongoing evaluation and improvement. A successful mentoring program that promotes mentor and mentee growth as well as increases student achievement can be developed by using the resources throughout this book (e.g., the special education mentor training described in Resource D).

Table 3.1 includes a mentoring program checklist to be used by program developers to ensure thoroughness in program planning. Each area is discussed in greater detail in this chapter.

CEC Mentoring Induction Program Description. The Council for Exceptional Children (CEC) was part of a three-year federally funded grant to develop a Mentoring Induction Project (MIP) and a draft report of the Mentoring Induction Principles and Guidelines are available at the CEC Web site: http://www.cec.sped.org/spotlight/udl/mip_g_manual_11pt.pdf.

The MIP principles and guidelines were developed, in part, by CEC to help school districts' efforts to find appropriately trained teachers and retain currently employed teachers. Attrition of teachers occurs at an alarming rate in special education and in order to ensure first-year teachers return for a second year, most school districts offer a generic new teacher mentoring and induction

Table 3.1   Mentoring program checklist

Activity:	Date Completed:	Notes:
• Develop goals and expected outcomes for mentoring program		
• Review policies to enable program to operate		Fiscal and contractual constraints Responsibilities of teachers
• Develop role and responsibilities of stakeholders		Mentor Mentee Administrator
• Generate options for recognition of mentors		
• Develop & enact mentor recruitment plan		
• Develop mentor support plan		Semester and year plans
• Establish timeline for mentoring activities		Beginning, mid-, and year-end activities
• Develop and present mentor training workshop, or personalize training workshop in Resource D		
• Match mentors to mentees		Consider geography, program level, number of mentors available, e-mentoring options available
• Plan and offer first meeting as a social event for all mentors and mentees to meet		
• Present mid-year and end-of-year mentoring program activities		
• Collect data for the mentoring program evaluation		
• Evaluate the mentoring program based on goals and outcomes set in Step 1		

Figure 3.1   Mentoring Induction Project conceptual model

MENTORING INDUCTION PROJECT CONCEPTUAL MODEL

SUPPORT

KNOWLEDGE			TEACHING SKILLS
SCHOOL	COMMUNITY	SPECIAL ED	Teaching Strategies
			Lesson Planning
Faculty	Resources	Due Process	Curricular Adaptations
Resources	Parents	Referrals	Inclusion Techniques
Schedules	Materials	IEPs	Classroom Management
Policy	Personal Needs	Evaluations	
Administrators	Entertainment	LRE	
Materials		Materials	
Culture		Curriculum	
Self-Esteem	Respect Collegiality	Self-Confidence	Professional Development
Job Satisfaction	Effective Teaching	Retention	Student Achievement

SOURCE: White & Mason (2003, p. 14). CEC Mentoring Induction Program.

program as a means of support. We advocate that school districts consider using a dedicated special education mentoring program or component to prepare new special education teachers for the nuances unique to special education.

The CEC Mentoring Induction Project is based on a conceptual framework that views support as an all-encompassing term which includes the knowledge and teaching skills required by new special education teachers as well as the influence of the school, community, and special education field. At the school level, a mentoring program needs to take into account variables including faculty, resources, schedules, policy, administrators, materials, and culture. Community variables related to successful new teacher induction include parents, materials, resources, personal needs, and entertainment. Special education variables related to teaching include due process, referrals, IEPs, evaluations, the least restrictive environment, materials, and curriculum. Each of these influences interact with teacher-specific variables such as self-esteem, job satisfaction, self-confidence, professional development, respect, collegiality, and student achievement. The MIP guidelines offer general suggestions for developing a special education mentoring program but do not provide detailed practicalities and how-to materials and resources needed to jump-start a mentoring program (see Figure 3.1).

According to White and Mason (2003), the six primary MIP guidelines are:

1. The objectives of the mentoring program, its purposes, and options are clear and have been agreed upon by beginning teachers, experienced mentors, and representatives from district- and building-level administrators.

2. Information concerning roles, expectations, policies, provisions, and desired outcomes of the mentoring program is readily available and shared with beginning teachers, mentors, and administrators.

3. The mentoring program is planned and adequately funded.

4. All first-year teachers are expected to participate in the mentoring program.

5. Mentoring for special education teachers may be coordinated with other, more general, mentoring programs within the school district, but must specifically address those issues unique to special education.

6. The mentoring program is designed to provide assistance and support only and is not related to any formal evaluations, certification requirements, or reemployment issues.

White and Mason (2003) further explains that, "The guidelines are based upon three basic principles:

1. An array of supports, including mentoring, should be available to all beginning teachers.

2. Effective mentoring relationships that provide meaningful supports to teachers are dependent upon several key components.

3. School districts have an obligation to ensure that their mentoring programs include those key components for effectiveness (p. 2).

The content of this book embodies the guidelines and points defined by the CEC and provides program designers with activities, resources, and applied tools that mentors and mentees need. Mentor and mentee roles and responsibilities are defined first.

ROLES AND RESPONSIBILITIES OF THE MENTOR AND MENTEE

The mentor-mentee match is one of the critical elements of a successful mentoring program because mentors provide more than just system information related to special education issues and instruction; mentors also provide emotional support. Mentees report that emotional support is one of the most valuable aspects a mentor provides (Whitaker, 2000a, Whitaker, 2000b). Providing emotional support helps reduce the isolation many new special education teachers experience during their first year of teaching. Often mentees are hesitant to ask for assistance, especially emotional assistance. Mentors offer this type of support by listening without judging, being sympathetic, and by being approachable and available to talk. Bova and Phillips (1981) offer characteristics found in any mentor-mentee relationship, two of which are particularly important for special education mentors:

1. The mentor-mentee relationship has a life cycle: introduction; mutual trust building; teaching of risk taking, communication, and professional skills; transfer of professional standards; and dissolution.

2. Mentor-mentee relationships end, amicably or bitterly.

The mentor has an opportunity to genuinely help another person and the relationship the mentor forms with the mentee is only as good as the effort invested into the relationship. Each mentor should strive to build a relationship that is mutually beneficial, ends amicably, and continues after the first year is complete.

The following are common roles and responsibilities of mentees and mentors compiled from several sources (Okeechobee New Teacher Support Manual, 2003; Southeast Regional Comprehensive System of Personnel Development, 2002; White & Mason, 2003).

New Special Education Teacher

Roles and Responsibilities

- Remain open to mentor feedback and suggestions

- Participate in the Teacher Support Program (or similar district program)

- Complete the mentor-mentee action plan

- Observe mentor and other teachers

- Meet with school administrator as needed

- Recognize and request assistance when needed

- Attend scheduled monthly inservice meetings

- Attend scheduled large-group informational meetings

- Communicate on a weekly basis with mentor teacher

- Provide documentation for new teacher development portfolio (if required)

Mentor Teacher

Roles and Responsibilities

- Review the school district policies and school handbook with the developing teacher

- Provide the new teacher with a copy of the Special Programs and Procedures manual

- Review school-based emergency drill plans

- Provide introductions and "who's who" tour for the new special education teacher

- Review lesson plans for proper format, reflection of course requirements and standards

- Review grading policies and school specific regulations

- Conference with the developing teacher at least once per week

- Make a monthly classroom visit to observe

- Serve as a mentor, friend, and guide for the developing teacher

- Assist your mentee with preparations for the first day of school

- Provide sustained support for the mentee

- Be a role model in all aspects of professionalism

- Be an active listener

- Give feedback on the program so future improvements can be made

- Maintain professional and confidential relationship

- Participate in evaluation of program

The benefits of mentoring should be presented to mentors to give them a clear understanding of ways they will benefit from their effort. Rewards for mentors may include tangible items as well as intrinsic rewards. Tangible rewards include recognition within the school district at a banquet, release time, extra materials, paid attendance to conferences, and possibly a stipend. Intrinsic rewards are more internal rewards such as feelings of increased confidence in their ability to provide support to others, increased job satisfaction, and knowing you made a difference in another teacher's life. Special education mentoring program designers should build both tangible and intrinsic rewards into their mentoring program.

ROLES AND RESPONSIBILITIES OF THE SCHOOL ADMINISTRATOR

Administrative support is critical to the success of new special education teachers (White & Mason, 2001). A perceived lack of support from administrators contributes to new special education teachers leaving the classroom or school. A lack of administrative support may lead to a discontentment as well as professional dissatisfaction and isolation.

The role of the special education administrator in supporting special education teachers varies from school to school. General roles and responsibilities for school administrators include:

- Demonstrate support, understanding, and encouragement

- Provide release time for beginning teachers and mentors to meet

- Conduct a diagnostic observation or conference with the new special education teacher

- Provide feedback and suggestions for improvement

- Coordinate all facets of The New Teacher Action Plan at the school level

- Meet with the mentor to discuss the progress of the developing teacher

- Schedule periodic meetings based upon the needs of the developing teacher

- Periodically check the developing teacher's portfolio

- Reduce responsibilities of beginning teachers

- Reduce responsibilities of mentors to allow the mentor to more easily meet with his or her mentee

- Participate in evaluation of the program

- Make informal contact with the mentoring pair at least once per month (e.g., phone, e-mail, or in person)

- Explain the new special education teacher's responsibility for attending faculty meetings

- Provide opportunities for the mentee to visit other classrooms and network with other special education personnel

- Support the new special education teacher's participation in professional organizations and associations

MENTOR SELECTION

The mentor-mentee match is often made by an administrator: the school principal or district special education director and staff. We recommend that the person who knows the mentor and mentee best make the matching decision because matching mentors and mentees is an art more than an exact science. Variables such as personality, teaching styles, student characteristics, and geographic locations all influence the administrator's decision-making process. Whitaker (2000a) reports that, based on previous research, between one-third and one-half of mentors assigned to mentees are not special education teachers. These data are alarming because experienced special education teachers should be mentoring new special education teachers. If there are not two special education teachers in the same school, the mentee should have two mentors: a generic mentor from the same school and a special education mentor from a different school. The generic mentor can answer the mentee's questions related to school-based issues, and the special education mentor can support the mentee's special education needs. With the use of technology, as discussed below, the mentor and mentee can teach the same type of students, but at different schools. By using technology, the new special education teacher can be mentored by an experienced special education teacher who is teaching the same type of students.

According to the CEC Mentoring Induction Project (White & Mason, 2003), the following four points should be considered when selecting mentors:

1. Mentor teachers must be special education teachers, ideally teaching in the same school, with the same population of students at the same grade level. If that is not possible, then the grade level, population of students, or location of the mentor could be changed, in that order. In no case should the mentor teacher not be in special education.

2. Mentor teachers are volunteers showing a commitment to the success of the beginning teacher.

3. Mentor teachers have 3–5 years of successful special education teaching experience in their current district.

4. Mentor teachers are nominated as master teachers by their building administrators or other appropriate school personnel (p. 5).

Table 3.2 contains a mentor nomination form that is easily modifiable to distribute to all special education teachers in the school district.

When mentors are assigned to work with general education teachers they are typically chosen based on their proximity to the mentee. Many times the mentor and mentee teach the same grade level in the same school. The matching of mentor to mentee is not as convenient for special education teachers. In some instances the new special educator may be the only special education teacher in the school or they may be the only teacher of an intermediate autistic unit in the district. Finding a mentor who teaches in the same school and at the same level as the mentee may not be realistic. Other options need to be considered.

One option is to partner a special education mentee with a general education mentor who teaches in the same building as the mentee. This mentor can provide support to the mentee on school- or- area-specific issues. For example, an experienced teacher in an inner-city school can be an essential support for a new teacher regardless of the types of classroom where they teach. A mentee paired with an in-school general education mentor would also need a special education mentor who would provide the support that is uniquely related to special education processes and policies. This special education mentor could be located at another school and they could communicate via e-mail, instant messenger, or telephone.

Another option is to make use of e-mentoring support. Later in this chapter we discuss ways to use e-mentoring as a way to support new teachers.

Ideally, the new special education teacher should be told about their mentor assignment in a face-to-face meeting with their administrator. This personal contact permits the new special education teacher to ask questions and gain a sense of administrative support. The administrator can describe the mentor's qualities and characteristics and help to reassure the new special education teacher that a successful and supportive experience is in everyone's best interest. The administrator can also give the new teacher a written document (see Table 3.3) noting their mentor and the mentor's contact information.

Additionally, the administrator should give the mentor a similar form (see Table 3.4) that contains pertinent information about the mentee, including name, contact phone number, and room and teaching assignment. If the

Table 3.2   Nomination of mentor

Become a Special Education Mentor

Nominations are being accepted for the Special Education Mentoring Program. The Mentor Teacher Program is designed to team experienced special education teachers with new special education teachers.

Mentor Nomination Criteria

Mentor teacher nominees exhibit the following:

1. Belief that all students can learn and that teachers can make it happen.

2. Effective classroom management skills.

3. Ability to design and use an individual behavior plan.

4. Planning that connects lesson plans to IEPs, curriculum, state standards, and assessment.

5. Interest in supporting teacher colleagues.

6. Good interpersonal skills.

7. Certification or licensing in special education.

8. At least three years of certified or licensed teaching experience in the area.

Mentor Responsibilities

The mentor teacher will do the following:

1. Attend a training session.

2. Invite the special education teacher to visit his or her classroom.

3. Visit the special education teacher's classroom.

4. Provide peer consultation regarding instructional and operational best practices.

5. Be assigned specific teachers for whom they will regularly observe, conduct postconferences, and provide insight and feedback to improve the effectiveness of the teacher's performance.

6. Support participant growth, model effective instructional techniques, monitor progress and activities, document observations, and maintain logs and records, while maintaining confidentiality and integrity of the information.

7. Identify and secure resources to assist participants as needed.

Table 3.2 (Continued)

Mentor Rewards May Include

1. Increased confidence in your ability to provide support to others.

2. Increased job satisfaction.

3. Knowing you made a difference in another teacher's life.

4. Recognition by peers as a valued member of the teaching community.

5. Additional release time or materials.

6. Stipend.

7. Payment for conference registration.

Mentor Nominations

Nominee _____   School _____

Nominated by: _____   School _____

Please return the completed form to: _____ no later than _____.

mentor receives a stipend, release time, materials, or other compensation for his or her efforts, it can be included in the assignment notification letter as well.

MENTOR TRAINING

Mentoring program designers should offer a dedicated workshop to teach the skills needed for effective mentoring. Just because a teacher is regarded as an effective teacher does not mean that teacher is a good mentor. The skills needed for mentoring another adult are very different from the skills used when working with children. Not all good special education teachers make good mentors. We recommend using the materials in Resource D as the foundation of a mentoring workshop.

The mentor training workshop in Resource D is designed to be delivered using multiple formats. The mentor's training can be offered in several short blocks, a one-day format, or a two-day format. The advantage to offering the workshop at the beginning of the school year in a one- or two-day format is that mentors receive all foundational information prior to working with their mentee. On the other hand, providing short blocks of training and ongoing support to mentors over the course of a year allows the mentors to receive the foundational information over time as well as meet periodically to discuss issues

Table 3.3   Mentee-mentor assignment

Mentee-Mentor

Teacher Assignment Notification

DATE:

TO:

SCHOOL:

FROM:

Welcome to our school district! We value you as a new special education teacher and strive to ensure your first year with us is successful. Our school district has a new special education teacher mentoring program in place to support you during the school year. Careful consideration has been given to your mentor so that you will be paired with another teacher who has experience working with similar students. Your mentor is aware of your assignment and has agreed to work closely with you during this school year. We know you will have a lot of questions and a lot to learn during this year, and with the help of your mentor, school, district staff, and the exceptional student education office, you will be successful.

_____   _____

Mentee   Mentor

_____   _____

Phone/e-mail address   Phone/e-mail address
Cc:

related to mentoring in their school or district. The workshop components and activities are flexible enough so that program developers can fine-tune the content to their school district's particular needs.

Components. The mentor's training provides the tools mentors need to be effective when working with the new special education teacher. Most teachers who want to become mentor teachers need guidance and information about the skills of effective mentors. Mentor teachers are usually the type of teachers who are willing to learn how to become an excellent mentor. They are receptive to becoming an effective problem solver, a cognitive coach, and an active listener. The workshop begins by asking mentor teachers to reminisce about their first days as a teacher and discuss their distinct memories in small groups. Next, teachers are taught about the phases of a teacher's first year, including the anticipation, survival, disillusionment, rejuvenation, and reflection phases. Skills for effective communication techniques are reviewed, including information about working with different personality styles. In the ensuing activity, each group of mentor teachers then discusses and creates their own "perfect" mentor.

Table 3.4   Mentee-mentor assignment

Mentor-Mentee Assignment Notification

DATE:

TO:

SCHOOL:

FROM:

Thank you for volunteering to mentor a new special education professional. We appreciate the time you are giving to help ensure the mentee's first year is successful. Careful consideration has been given to the mentor-mentee match so that you will be paired with a new teacher with similar students. Your mentee is aware of your assignment and has reviewed his or her roles and responsibilities. Once again, thank you for your dedication to the profession.

_____   _____
Mentee   Mentor

_____   _____
Phone/e-mail address   Phone/e-mail address
Cc:

The workshop then focuses on reflective listening techniques followed by an activity to practice effective listening. Cognitive coaching is reviewed along with effective problem solving and practice scenarios. Mentor teachers then learn four ways they can support new special education teachers, including low- and high-intensity types of supports. The last part of the workshop addresses creating a mentor-mentee action plan with measurable goals and action steps as well as action plan outcomes. The mentors are taught how to fade support, also known as supportive release. The workshop ends with how to evaluate the mentoring program.

Mentor Training Session (provided in Resource D). These skills and others are taught within the workshop in Resource D. Mentor teachers typically know the school district policies and procedures related to special education so this type of information is not provided in our workshop but the workshop format is flexible enough so program designers can easily infuse their district-specific information.

E-MENTORING

E-mentoring involves the use of distance technology (e-mail, text, audio or video conferencing) to communicate and support the mentoring relationship. With increasing technological capabilities, more teachers are communicating in ways other than face-to-face meetings. Often mentors and mentees in the same school find using e-mail a more efficient way to communicate because many classrooms do not have telephones and teachers are unable to leave their students to ask their mentor a question. Given the rapid expansion of technology, many school districts have established or are pilot testing e-mentoring programs. The continuing growth, expansion, and development of user-friendly e-mentoring technologies is expected.

How to E-Mentor. Lloyd, Wood, and Moreno (2000) report that some mentors and mentees keep in touch using e-mail if they are not at the same school. E-mail is a viable way for a mentor and mentee who teach the same types of children (e.g., children with severe autism), to share singular challenges when working in different geographic locations. In the majority of school districts, e-mail is readily available and teachers are familiar with using it. E-mentoring also includes online chats. Live chats allow instant responses and clarification of concerns. Online bulletin boards or message boards are another way the mentor and mentee can connect if the technology for online chats is unavailable. The mentee can post a message and the mentor then reads and responds.

Some school districts offer the mentor and mentee video conferencing via the Internet. To use video conferencing, the mentor and mentee must have broadband Internet in their classrooms connected to a video. According to Andres (1993), President of Global SchoolNet, "Video conferencing over the Internet requires substantial bandwidth and a powerful desktop computer. Video conferencing allows for experiences and interactivity that would not be possible through any other medium. It's better than television, and not quite as good as 'live and in person.'" Andres elaborates that a video conference is like a meeting that functions best when there is an agenda and a moderator. The moderator is important to consider using when there are multiple people on the same video conference or when a newly trained mentor wants some feedback on his or her mentor skills. The Web site http://www.gsn.org/cu/videoconf.html offers tips on hosting an effective Internet video conference including topics such as lighting, eye contact, audio, interactivity, appearance and attention, and photos and props.

Each school or district e-mentoring program should be designed to meet the particular needs of the mentors and mentees, so most programs are not identical. For example, some rural school districts use advanced technology because resources are not in close proximity, whereas larger districts have funding barriers to implementing a district-wide e-mentoring program. Key stakeholders from special education and technology can consider guiding questions located in the following list during the exploration and design phase of e-mentoring.

E-mentoring Guiding Questions

- What are the technology capacities at the school?

- Is equipment available (computers, video-conferencing hardware, etc.)?

- Is the focus of the mentoring to provide expert advice in a question-and-answer format or will it only involve one-to-one communication?

- What timeline is expected for a response when using e-mail?

- Should or could e-mail or other communication be monitored by a third party?

- How will teacher and student confidentiality be protected?

- Will the mentor be proactive or reactive to the mentee's needs?

Benefits and Drawbacks. Research has validated the visible results of many face-to-face mentoring programs. Whereas there have been a number of case students and some evaluation studies, e-mentoring programs are relatively new. In rural districts e-mentoring is advantageous to help bridge the distance gap that may occur between schools, districts, or universities. Additionally, in special education, e-mentoring can bring together teachers who are the sole special education teacher at their school. Other potential benefits of e-mentoring include reducing the long-distance barriers when mentors work in different geographic locations, pairing mentors and mentees with the same teaching assignments who without the use of technology would not be associated, reducing costs associated with long-distance telephone calling, and the ability to have instant communication access at any time.

A disadvantage of electronic mentoring is that the mentor-mentee pair may never or only infrequently meet in person. The convenience of e-mail may cause the pair to rely on technology as the only form of contact. It is unclear if this causes the relationships to be less intense or less supportive. Paul Riede describes in his 2003 article, the outcomes of a triadic mentoring model used by a superintendent and two fledgling principals. Riede describes the electronic mentoring model used to connect principals a hundred miles away from the central office. Fortunately, his analysis of the three-year e-mentoring relationship indicated that the closeness and camaraderie expected in a mentoring relationship was not compromised by the electronic communication.

Another drawback is that it may be hard to sustain an e-mentoring relationship when the mentor and mentee have never met face-to-face. In addition, matching teachers from other geographic locations is challenging and difficult if the administrator does not know a great deal about the mentor or mentee. Of course, when the technology is dated or inadequate to support e-mentoring these types of mentoring supports are limited. These e-mentoring benefits and drawbacks serve as a starting point for discussing each school district's technology capabilities as they relate to mentoring. Debby Brown shared her experience mentoring a special education teacher in a different school.

> I am the mainstream consultant at an elementary school. The teacher I mentored was at the high school in an intellectually disabled classroom. I spoke with him a few times at the beginning of the year to help him with some advice on how to communicate with his new team members. We reconnected again using e-mail every few months and he seemed to be doing very well in his new position. Each time I made contact he assured me things were going well. It was difficult to mentor someone not in my building but the use of technology helped the distance. At the end of the year he thanked me for taking the time to support him when he needed advice.

Table 3.5   Conference log

Mentoring Conference Log

Date:	
Time:	
Location (circle one): in person, phone, e-mail, video conference, online chat, other	
Notes:	
Follow-up:	

Regardless of whether the mentor and mentee meet face-to-face or via e-mentoring, the conference should be documented. Documentation from the conference provides the mentor and mentee with notes related to current concerns and positive outcomes. Conference notes may also be used to highlight the mentee's professional growth during his or her first year. Conference notes provide data for the mentee's professional development plan and show progress on the action plan objectives. Although the conference notes can be used as part of the mentoring program evaluation at the end of the year, the mentor and mentee should ensure that the notes are not used in any way to evaluate the mentee's performance in the interest of confidentiality. Table 3.5 contains a sample mentoring conference log.

MENTORING ACTIVITIES CALENDAR

The mentoring activities timeline located in Resource E provides a concise overview of activities the mentor and mentee may complete during the school year. The activities timeline starts with the first month of school and contains activities that mentors can complete monthly. During the beginning months of school there are more activities the special education mentor and mentee should complete and the activities gradually subside as the new special education teacher gains confidence and the mentor begins to fade support. If the mentor creates a notebook for the mentee, the activities calendar is a useful tool to include.

ACTION PLANNING

Implementation. The development of a mentor-mentee action plan was discussed in detail in Chapter 1 and is briefly reviewed again. The action plan serves as a tool for helping the mentee identify and make progress toward enhancing his or her teaching skills (See Resources A and D for sample action plans). An action plan is a collaboratively designed document used for the benefit of the mentor and mentee to focus on common goals, define responsibilities, and chronicle the mentee's professional progress. Additionally, the action plan is a working document that is revised and modified as needed.

Concerns. Mentors can relate the mentee's action plan to a student's IEP. The action plan, like the IEP, is a useful tool when used properly. If the mentor and mentee keep the plan accessible and review it at least biweekly, the plan will be put to use and steps will be taken to achieve the goals, similar to their student's IEP. On the other hand, if the action plan remains filed in a drawer and only removed at the end of the school year, the plan is worthless; just as a student's IEP would be useless if not reviewed during the school year. The benefits of using the action plan are well worth the initial investment of time and outweigh any limitations. However, the final decision to use or ignore the action planning process rests with the school district, mentor, and mentee. Program designers should emphasize the merits of action planning.

Fading Support. Mentoring is a process and knowing when to end the process is often a difficult decision. The mentor has worked along with the mentee to teach them independence in all areas of special education. From managing student behavior and writing IEPs to listening to a frustrating experience, the mentor has diligently supported the new special education teacher. In the ideal situation, the mentor and mentee mutually agree that the mentee has the confidence to handle all things related to teaching. This does not mean the mentee suddenly seizes asking questions or can solve every problem independently. It does mean that the mentee has the "with-it-ness" to recognize and solve most problems and knows who to consult if the problem cannot be solved alone. It means the mentor has completed the job. In the next vignette, Kathy Huie, an experienced mentor, described one situation that signaled to her that the mentee "got it."

> For most of the first half of the semester, I would walk around Christina's classroom while she was teaching or the kids were working, and when I spotted misbehavior on the part of the kids, I would signal her or walk over to her and say, "Look back there in the corner . . ." or "What's going on with those boys over there?" Then, she would go handle whatever situation I had spotted.
>
> One day, after the middle of the semester, I walked into Christina's class for my daily visit. The class was busy working in their seats, and Christina was working at her desk. I sat down next to her, and we started catching up on her day. Suddenly, Christina raised her head and looked across the room. "Just a minute," she said to me. "There's something going on over there. I've got to see what it is." She got up and went across the room to deal with students who were off task— misbehavior that I hadn't even spotted.
>
> As I watched her go, I thought, "She's going to be OK." She had taken ownership of her class and had developed her radar or "with-it-ness"

enough to see problems on her own and deal with them on her own. She didn't need me anymore and I began to fade my support. (Kathy Huie)

Situations as clear as Kathy's do not always happen but the typical process for fading support is to fade one support at a time. For example, the mentor might fade the mentee's classroom-based situational support and provide consultative support as needed during their planning time. After the mentor faded all professional support, he or she would begin to fade social support as needed. But for many mentors and mentees the shared experiences create a social bond that spans beyond the first year of teaching.

FUNDING MENTORING PROGRAMS

Funding is always a top issue when developing a new program. Funding for special education mentoring programs can come from many sources including community organizations, foundations, consortiums, partnerships, discretionary grants, school district, and state funding. An Internet search using the search words "special education mentor funding" reveals numerous leads for program developers to follow in order to secure external funding. One site that has mentor funding opportunities is the National Education Association (NEA) (http://www .nfie.org/). Guidelines for applying for grants are available on the NEA Web site.

The Education Commission of the States (1999) reviewed variables related to student achievement and recommended that teacher preparation and professional development include the creation and funding of mentoring programs for beginning teachers. This recommendation was based on evidence that mentoring dramatically increases the retention rate of new teachers. Their report highlights the fact that many states are presently considering legislation to establish or expand beginning teacher mentoring programs. At the time, Michigan did not have any state dollars allocated for mentoring programs and local districts had to provide professional development activities and mentors. Program developers can check this Web site to determine if funding is available in their state as well as refer to Resource B.

Susan Villani (2002) wrote a book on various models of mentoring programs for new teachers which contains information on funding mentoring programs. She profiles generic mentoring programs from around the United States and has chapters related to school system- or district-funded programs, state-funded programs, grant-funded programs, and alternatively funded programs. This is a worthwhile resource for special education mentoring program developers to review when researching funding sources.

Our mentoring program is funded by the Comprehensive System of Personnel Development (CSPD) and each of the partners contributes resources to the program. School district personnel and faculty from the local university contributed their time and resources and collaboratively developed the mentoring program. Funding from the CSPD grant pays for the workshop facilitator, small stipends to the mentors, and for a Web site containing mentoring resources and a discussion board. Each school district contributes their staff time to provide ongoing support to mentors and mentees. Our program is in its second year and special education teacher retention rates have increased within our school districts.

Evaluating the effectiveness of mentoring programs is important given the current environment of data, documentation, and difficult fiscal budgets. Documentation is useful when school boards and funding agencies require data showing that mentoring is useful. Mentoring program designers typically have little control over the primary variables influencing teacher turnover, including school district salary, administrator support, and teaching conditions, yet they can influence variables related to the mentoring program's design. Mentor selection, matching, workshop content, and ongoing mentor-mentee support are variables typically within the program developer's influence.

So who should evaluate the special education mentoring program? All key stakeholders can be involved in evaluating the mentoring program's effectiveness. Program designers, mentors, mentees, and principals are some key stakeholders that have direct experience with the program. Additionally, the district's special education department may also take part in coordinating the program's evaluation to determine successes or shortfalls. Each group of stakeholders has a slightly different perspective, each of which provides useful decision-making information. Data from each perspective should be gathered and synthesized to answer each mentoring program evaluation question.

How should the special education mentoring program be evaluated? "Always keep data," is advice offered by Education World, a Web site containing extensive teacher resources on mentoring and other educational topics. Data can be collected via surveys, interviews, focus groups, action plans, and from student records, such as report cards. Key stakeholders should consider these questions when deciding which data is needed to evaluate and document the effectiveness of the special education mentoring program.

School Administrators

- What are the mentee and mentor's satisfaction levels?

- What are the retention rates of new special education teachers? In our district? In the mentee's school?

- Did student achievement increase?

- Were parents satisfied with the new teacher?

- What were the goals of the mentoring program that were met?

- Does program funding need to be increased or decreased?

- Were mentors supported during the school year?

- Are there other indicators?

Mentors

- Have the mentee's action plan goals been satisfied?

- How did the mentor grow professionally?

- Were the mentor's needs met during the school year?

- What did the mentor learn the most about? The least?

- Other indicators?

Mentees

- Have the action plan goals been satisfied?

- Were the mentee's needs met?

- Why did the mentee remain in the teaching position?

- Why did the mentee leave the teaching position?

- Was the mentee supported at the school level? District level?

- Are there other indicators?

Each data source can answer individual questions that contribute to the complete program evaluation. The data should not be used solely to determine if the program should be continued or not, but it is most useful for identifying solid areas of the program as well as those areas needing strengthening. As outlined in the designing-mentoring-program steps found at the beginning of this chapter, stakeholders should set goals and outcomes prior to implementing the mentoring program. Evaluating the program based on your preset goals and outcomes is a logical method for evaluation. Just remember, program evaluation is an ongoing process to reflect on the progress of the mentor, mentee, principal, and everyone involved in designing and implementing the special education mentoring program.

WHAT IF?

What if our school district does not have enough special education mentors to support new special education teachers? Should we hire retired special education teachers?

Possible responses include the following:

- We feel fine hiring retired special education teachers to fill the role of the mentor teacher and have used retired teachers in our mentoring program very successfully. It is still important to keep in mind the same critical elements as discussed in Chapter 3, such as ensuring the retired special education teacher completes a mentor workshop, there is a careful match between the mentor and mentee so that, before retiring, the mentor taught the same types of students as the mentee. Make sure the retired mentor is clear about the time commitment required for successful mentoring and is willing to come to the school, attend workshops or conferences, and, if needed, provide support outside of school. The mentor should also be skilled with technology and using e-mail to communicate with the mentee.

- We would be concerned with hiring a retired special education teacher as a mentor if he or she had lost touch with best practices or legislative changes in special education.

ONLINE RESOURCES FOR DESIGNING MENTORING PROGRAMS

Table 3.6   Online resources for designing mentoring programs

Web site	Description
www.inspiringteachers.com	Contains a Mentor Teachers Page. The Web site is a community of educators with the mission of empowering new teachers for classroom success.
www.teachers.net	*Contents:* • Harry Wong column • Chat center • Teachers.net fundraising • Free lesson plans • Live meetings • Live chatroom • Teacher jobs • Classroom centers • Classroom projects • Distance learning • Teacher mailings • Teacher chatboards
www.iearn.org/circles/mentors.html	*Contents:* • Examples of tele-mentoring projects • Ask an expert • Pair mentoring • Group mentoring • Design issues in creating tele-mentoring programs • Tele-mentoring human resources • Matching challenges • The nature of the interaction • Reciprocity • Sustainability • Tele-mentoring resources
http://www.teachers-first.com/sped/prof/index.html	This valuable site provides teachers and other education professionals with information and resources about teaching students with disabilities.
http://www.tr.wou.edu/rrp/index.htm	This site describes the Oregon special education recruitment and retention project and is filled with resources.
www.teachermentors.com	This site contains Barry Sweeny's own best practices on mentoring.
http://www.unm.edu/~induct/	This site is run by the University of New Mexico and contains tips and hot topics of interest to support new special educators.

(Continued)

Table 3.6 (Continued)

Web site	Description
http://www.mentors.net/03articles.html	This is the site of the Mentoring Leadership and Resource Network. It began as a grassroots effort started by a few educators with a goal to increase the knowledge base and general awareness of the best practices in the mentoring and induction of new teachers.
www.ecs.org/clearinghouse/13/15/1315.doc	This site contains information on states that have or are considering legislation to establish or expand beginning teacher mentoring (1999).

REFERENCES

Andres, Y. M. (1993). *Elements of an effective internet video conference.* Retrieved January 14, 2004, from http://www.gsn.org/cu/videoconf.html

Billingsley, B. (1993). Teacher retention and attrition in special education and general education: A critical review of research. *Journal of Special Education, 27*(2), 137–173.

Bova, B. M., & Phillips, R. E. (1981). *The mentor relationship: A study of mentors and protégés in business and academia.* (Report No. CE 030362). New Mexico. (ERIC Document Reproduction Service No. ED 208233)

Council for Exceptional Children. (2000). *What every special educator must know: The international standards for the preparation and certification of special education teachers* (4th ed.). Reston, VA: Author.

Education Commission of the States. (1999). *Beginning Teacher Mentoring Programs.* Retrieved on July 29, 2004, from http://www.ecs.org/clearinghouse/13/15/1315.doc

Lloyd, S. R., Wood, T. A., & Moreno, G. (2000). What's a mentor to do? *Teaching Exceptional Children, 33*(1), 38–42.

Miller, M. D., Brownell, M. T., & Smith, S. W. (1999). Factors that predict teachers staying in, leaving, and transferring from the special education classroom. *Exceptional Children, 65*(2), 201–218.

Okeechobee County School District. (2003). *Teacher mentoring handbook.* Okeechobee, FL: Author.

Oregon Special Education Recruitment and Retention Project. (2002). *Implementing Mentoring Programs.* Retrieved June 25, 2002, from http://www.tr.wou.edu/rrp/mentext.htm

Riede, P. (2003). Electronic mentoring. *School Administrator, 66*(10), 26–29.

Southeast Regional Comprehensive System of Personnel Development. (2002). *A two-day mentoring workshop.* Florida Atlantic University: Author.

Villani, S. (2002). *Mentoring programs for new teachers: Models of induction and support.* Thousand Oaks, CA: Corwin Press.

Whitaker, S. D. (2000a). What do first-year special education teachers need? *Teaching Exceptional Children, 33*(1), 28–36.

Whitaker, S. D. (2000b). Mentoring beginning special education teachers and the relationship to attrition. *Exceptional Children, 66*(4), 546–566.

White, M., & Mason, C. (2001). The mentoring induction project: Supporting beginning special education professionals—curriculum concerns of new teachers. *Teaching Exceptional Children, 34*(2), 89.

White, M., & Mason, C. (2003). *Mentoring induction principles and guidelines.* Reston, VA: CEC Publications. U. S. Department of Education (OSEP Grant # H32N99900047).

Becoming a Mentor 4

VIGNETTE

I have thought about your question, "What helped you the most your first year of teaching?" That is very hard to pinpoint since it was a whole school of things.

First, I was assigned a mentor teacher. She made me feel as if no question was too stupid. Her advice and sharing of supplies, professional magazines, and books was extremely helpful. I also met and followed around a very positive teacher who to me appeared confident, conscientious, and dressed for success, very professional. I tried to always use confident body language even though at times I felt like crying, it really helped!

—Margaret Hearndon

WHO SHOULD BE A MENTOR?

The quick answer to that question is a mentor should have about three years experience in the field in which they mentor. They should be certified by the state to teach in that field and be seen by their evaluators as "excellent teachers." That's the easy answer. At many elementary schools there may be only one experienced special education teacher. That does not mean, however, they will assuredly be "excellent." When the pool to select from is very shallow, we have to consider other options. Let us first consider what makes a good mentor, and then we will explore ways to find them.

Skills Needed by Mentors. James Rowley (1999) worked with the National Mentoring Leadership and Resource Network for many years before he collected and published his basic yet essential characteristics of mentors. He developed his list of qualities by listening to mentors and mentees across the country. In his article in *Educational Leadership,* he describes these qualities:

"Qualities of a Good Mentor"

The good mentor is committed to the role of mentoring.

The good mentor is accepting of the beginning teacher.

The good mentor is skilled in providing instructional support.

The good mentor is effective in interpersonal contexts.

The good mentor is a model of a continuous learner.

The good mentor communicates hope and optimism. (pp. 20–22)

Finding Good Mentors. Rowley identified commitment as the first quality. He proposes that the good mentors must communicate to their mentees that they as mentors intend to persist and that new teachers need to persist as well. When veterans talk about their early experiences in education, not all are rosy recollections. Some are very scary. They tell tales of not feeling prepared, of doing everything exactly the wrong way. Yet they kept at it and tried new things to make the process of teaching better. They persisted. This is crucial for new teachers to hear, and who better to tell them but those teachers who know you "have to try new things" and that "the first time isn't always the right way." Good mentors communicate the idea that they are committed to teaching and to mentoring as a way to make the process of teaching better. They choose to mentor just as they chose to persist in improving teaching.

A good mentor knows the new teacher is coming from a different place than they are. However, they also know that the new teacher is coming from the same place that they once came. This is part of understanding the frame of reference we all possess. Understanding frame of reference is essential to working with other people. If you understand "where a person is coming from," then you are more likely to be able to communicate with him or her. Further, if your goal is to make a change in behaviors, then understanding another's frame of reference will allow you to determine how much change is acceptable. A study published by Richardson, Anders, Tidwell, and Lloyd (1991) used the idea of frame of reference to change teachers' reading instruction practices. They employed a beliefs interview at the beginning of the study and keyed in on specific words, concepts, and techniques that the teachers referred to in describing their philosophy of reading. Then the research team attempted to identify what the teachers' beliefs really were and what they could offer the teachers to help improve their teaching. Their goal was to offer ideas that fit the teachers' frames of reference. For example, if they talked about language and reading being contextually bound, they would not think of offering to show them innovative phonics techniques. The ideas the researchers offered where usually incorporated because they fit their conception of good reading instruction.

The notion of a frame of reference is especially important when working with a new teacher. It has been a long time since veteran teachers have felt the fear of a new teacher. When an experienced teacher walks into a classroom, he or she knows what to accomplish and how to get there. If a student throws a curve, the veteran can usually pull something out of his or her "bag of tricks" to suit the situation. It is a little different with new teachers. They too only know what they have observed or experienced in the past. The difference is that those observations and experiences may have been minimal, so their "bag of tricks" is very limited. They approach many seemingly typical teaching situations with trepidation. Put yourself in their shoes and think how you might react. Before providing feedback or support the mentor has to view the situation as a new teacher might (i.e., he or she has to step into the new teacher's frame of reference).

Think about how important this is when we are working in multicultural settings. Understanding the cultural perspective of another person is crucial for effective communication. This story from a community college instructor describes how frame of reference plays into communication and personal relationships.

I taught in Arizona for several years while I was working on my doctorate and encountered several students from different tribes of Native Americans. One young woman from the Pima tribe was in my study skills class at the community college. Every day I would greet her and the rest of the students when they came into class. The others would respond with a "hi" or smile. She, however, would enter my classroom, move to her seat, get her materials out and then finally make eye contact with me. It was not until she came to class early one day when she asked me to wait to talk with her until she got herself ready. She needed time to get ready before she could deal with my greetings. I was stunned. She went on to say that in her culture, people of respect do not usually begin the conversations with others. They usually wait until the younger person started talking. I thought she was just being shy, so I tried harder to get her to interact. My frame of reference made her behavior seem different to me, just as my behavior seemed odd to her.

Ellen Moir (1999) wrote about keeping in mind that new teachers go through phases during their induction year and a mentor's attention to these phases will ultimately make the mentoring process more effective. She identified five phases that teachers go through during their first year of teaching. The first phase is *Anticipation Phase.* This phase begins during student teaching, just as the assignments are finishing up and the student can actually see herself as a teacher next year. This excitement revolves around making a commitment to making a difference. It also includes romanticizing the role of the teacher. Idealism and excitement characterize the first few weeks of the school year. The excitement of this phase is increased when the recent graduates get their first job and their first class assignment. The beginning of the year for special education teachers is a process of learning the students, learning the school, and learning the curriculum. The mentee approaches these learning tasks with great enthusiasm. Mentors are most helpful to mentees in the anticipation phase when they begin to share the best ways to access information. During this phase, mentors and mentees are typically getting to know each other; so celebrating in the new job is a logical response.

By October, new teachers have entered the second phase—that is, the *Survival Phase.* During this phase new teachers are overwhelmed with learning a "million" new things; some very *big* (like curriculum and management) and some very small (like bus duty and taking attendance). No matter how small, they all take on gargantuan proportions. The two biggest concerns for teachers at this phase are developing curriculum and saving face. Veteran teachers have old lessons and unit plans to draw from when developing teaching materials. New teachers are constantly making new things for every lesson. New teachers are moving forward at a breakneck pace. New teachers are concerned with how they are viewed by their fellow teachers and the administration. They may make many decisions based on how they are perceived by the principal—Am I sending too many students to the office? Do they think I don't know what I'm doing? I don't want them to know I'm scared! New special education teachers at this phase need their mentors to help the mentees reflect on how they are doing—how they are *really* doing. They can do this by sharing.

The third phase of a teacher's first year is the *Disillusionment Phase.* After about eight weeks of high-intensity stress, new teachers are plagued by thoughts of incompetence. They start making comments like "It shouldn't be this hard—maybe I'm not cut out for teaching." This is underscored by having to conduct parent conferences and not knowing how to describe their plan for the rest of the year. They may have difficulty planning for the rest of the week! Added to this is the toll the stress takes on new teachers' physical health. The only ray of hope during this phase is that winter break is near. Mentors provide the emotional support that will help the mentee get through the intervening weeks before a break becomes a reality.

The fourth phase is the *Rejuvenation Phase.* After winter break, the beginning of January signals an improvement in attitude. Like spring weather, the change is slow in coming, but a positive attitude does eventually make an appearance. The rejuvenation phase is not a smooth one; some ups and downs still occur. When year-end testing arrives, teachers again question themselves about their ability to be the best teacher for their students. The mentor has the ability to reassure the mentee that he or she is acting in the best interest of the students.

The final phase is the *Reflection Phase* and it begins during the last six weeks of school. Teachers begin to reflect on the year as a whole—not the small problems, but the whole picture. They begin to make plans for the next year, especially in the areas of management, curriculum, and teaching strategies. This reflection phase allows them to return to the anticipation phase they began the year with. Mentors, at this phase, are able to talk about what has gone well for their mentees and help them plan the next year's program.

Mentors will find it helpful to keep in mind the phases and needs within each phase when working with new teachers. As a veteran, you can tell they need help with management, but they may not be ready to hear that or ready to work on it. They have other things that seem more pressing, like the policies and procedures for the school or developing lesson plans. Successful mentors give the mentees what they need with priorities in mind and in a timely manner so that they can handle it.

Rowley continues with his *qualities of good mentors* by including the need for high-quality instructional support skills. The ability a mentor has to offer adequate instructional support truly depends on the way the mentoring program is designed. If a mentor and mentee only talk outside the classroom because they both have full-time responsibilities for teaching, then the support has to be given outside the classroom. Think how different it might be if the mentor was able to be in the mentee's class on a daily basis. Then mentor could teach, model, co-teach, think aloud, and so forth all for the benefit of the mentee. This may be more feasible for grade-level teachers as opposed to special education teachers. We are faced with the reality that some special education teachers teach alone in their school. There may not be the ideal mentor at their school, so the options for a mentor may be a general education teacher at their school or a special education teacher who teaches miles away. Before making the choice, consider who can spend the quality time with the new teacher to provide instructional support.

Personality Traits of Effective Mentors. Chapter 5 of this book describes the interpersonal communication skills needed by mentors. It cannot be stressed enough that the way we communicate with others is just as important as what we are saying. This is very true for the mentor/mentee relationship. The mentor has to think about how the information will "play" in the mind of the mentee. That is not to say that we should sugarcoat the message; rather, gauge the intent that will come along with the message.

Good mentors are models of lifelong learning. When the new year starts, teachers select from a menu of inservice activities or staff development opportunities. New teachers will not be able to discern which workshops would be helpful and which are crucial. Supportive mentors help protégés think through what they need and help prioritize the activities. Good mentors model their own desire to keep current and informed by having a history of attending conferences and workshops. In addition, they will invite their protégés to come along with them and build their own history of continual learning.

A good mentor communicates optimism. Who would want a mentor who is constantly looking at the dark side of any school activity? Certainly not a new, impressionable teacher; a retention-minded principal or special education director wouldn't either. The mentee often takes his or her cue from the mentor, so much so that the things the mentor disdains the mentee may not even try. Therefore, whereas it is not helpful to ignore realities, it is equally problematic to be forever pessimistic. Conversations in public and private between mentors and mentees should be realistic, with mentors sharing struggles and success they have experienced.

WHAT DO MENTORS DO?

There is a growing interest in developing mentor programs as a way to retain new teachers. The resources for developing mentor programs are varied and provide many ideas for how to develop programs, what the mentors should do, and how the mentors should be compensated. Of all the information included in these resources, one concept is common to the mentoring programs for general and special education alike. *A mentor is not an evaluator.* The mentor works with a teacher without the need or responsibility to evaluate. This relationship allows the mentee to talk, cry, confess to mistakes, and reveal fears. Imagine how the relationship would change if the mentor was also responsible for making a formative evaluation of the mentee!

If we start from the premise that whatever a mentor does (the roles and responsibilities will be described in more detail in a moment), it is not evaluative, then we have the ability to open the relationship between the mentor and mentee to a wide array of activities and ideas. If we limit the relationship by having the mentor provide evaluations to either the mentee or the administration, then the responsibilities take on a managerial or administrative nature.

Roles and Responsibilities of a Mentor. In a research brief for the Northwest Regional Educational Laboratory (2001), Cori Brewster and Jennifer Railsback (2001) provide a summary of the roles and responsibilities of a mentor that make a difference to new teachers' socialization to a school.

Mentor teachers assume the responsibility to:

- Share information about the program, procedures, guidelines, and expectations

- Link the mentee to the appropriate resources

- Act as a role model to the mentee

- Share teaching strategies and materials

- Offer professional and collegial support

- Provide guidance in discipline, planning, and scheduling

- Promote self-reflection and analysis (Brewster & Railsback, 2001)

The mentor's biggest role is socializing the mentee to the new setting. The responsibility for sharing programmatic or procedural information is often handled best by an individual who is teaching in the same area. The number of special education teachers varies from school to school; as does the likelihood that an experienced special education teacher at the same school can mentor a new special education teacher. Sometimes program developers have to look to special education teachers at nearby schools to provide the program-specific mentoring or even seek out general education teachers and counselors who have been special education teachers in the past.

A mentor chosen from beyond the immediate school environment entails the consideration of an additional on-site mentor. The on-site mentor can be an outstanding grade-level teacher who can assist in helping the new teacher learn the process at their specific school. In essence, one would socialize the mentee to ABC Elementary School and the other would socialize him or her to the district and special education policy.

- The last role listed in Brewster and Railsback's compilation is to help the mentee promote reflective practice. The mentor may have to place reflection on the back burner until the new teacher is ready to work on it. New teachers go through stages and microphases of concern during their first year of teaching. We have already looked at how emotional a new teacher's first year can be by looking at Moir's phases. The same can be said for the areas of concern for new teachers. Cheney, Krajewski, and Combs (1992) describe the concerns held by first-year teachers to be limited to the following:

- Order and time filling

- Timing, planning, and management

- Experimentation

- Long-range planning

- Focus on students (1992)

All these areas make appropriate jumping-off points for any mentor-mentee relationship. Needs expressed by new special education teachers become more specific after their first year of teaching. Susan Whitaker (2003) identified four areas of concern from teachers completing their first year in special education. These include:

- Learning special education policies, procedures, and paperwork

- Receiving emotional support

- Learning school-based procedures, and

- Learning where to find resources

Why are these needs different for special education teachers? It seems they have procedural needs that cannot often be met by the general orientation new teachers receive. They are also keenly aware that there are few people at each school who will know the answers to these questions. Whitaker went on to express that new special education teachers fear the needs they have (to find the answers to process questions) will not be met. They are often very eager to request support and are surprised when the information is not forthcoming.

WHAT DO MENTORS DO WHEN THE MENTORING RELATIONSHIP ISN'T WORKING?

This was my second year participating in the mentoring program. Unfortunately, I had another unsuccessful experience. In the summary I completed last year, I expressed how I felt it was difficult mentoring a person who is not open to the help and who is located at a different school. This proved to be true once again.

I made my initial contact with my beginning teacher through e-mail and later through the telephone. I was hopeful that this time things would be better. We talked on the phone for a while and I gave as many suggestions as I could to help her in her situation. She was struggling with a large number of students as well as a wide range of grade levels. We also discussed some of the recent obstacles she was facing. I primarily listened and offered advice when I felt I could. When I offered the advice, she was not very open to the suggestions. During our conversation, she informed me that she was no longer able to talk to anyone else and she would not be able to take my help this year. I offered to come out and help her, but she informed me that she was not allowed to have any visitors in her classroom. I continued to offer her help anytime she needed it, and I told her she could just e-mail me if she needed anything. I also gave her my home phone number. Throughout the year, I e-mailed her offering assistance and support. She kindly responded, but never asked for anything. I am sure this is a good program, but I have had two unsuccessful experiences. I think the person who is the beginning teacher needs to be open to having someone help them. (Jennifer Thomas)

Even the best-laid plans can go awry. Mentors can be trained and support may be planned; yet problems with the mentor-mentee match-up can be problematic. The typical problems observed in new mentor-mentee match-ups include:

- Mentee doesn't know he or she needs help

- Mentee and mentor can't seem to find the time to get together

- Personalities clash

- Mentee is asking too much of the mentor

The response of the mentor varies in each case. However, crucial to the problem-solving process is for the mentor to communicate with the mentoring program coordinator. These individuals provide a perspective that is less involved in the relationship. One mentor, Lisa Heinz, talks about mentoring and being "personally and professionally important." Even when Lisa's mentoring assignment didn't work out, she tried to help another new teacher. Someone who is that close to the conflict situation may not be able to step aside and think about possible solutions.

Let's examine the typical problems listed above and think about how to handle these situations.

Mentees Don't Know They Need Help

Some mentees are not able to look up from the preparation and teaching long enough to know what to ask. These mentees are in survival mode and are functioning from day to day. Mentors can respond to this type of problem by revisiting the mentee needs assessment to identify clearly the problem. Is this a classroom management issue? Is the mentee leaving exactly at 3:00 P.M., putting in minimal time on prep and reflection? Is the mentee working with too many students? The mentor's first job is to identify and prioritize needs; next, to provide support for the individual. The mentee's action plan may need revision to reflect the narrower focus.

Mentee and Mentor Can't Seem to Find the Time to Get Together

This problem may be the result of the mentor and mentee that are assigned to different schools. The mentor could do as Jennifer Thomas did and use electronic mentoring methods (phone, e-mail, etc.). If e-mentoring isn't possible, the mentor may need to approach the school administrator to ask for release time to visit the mentee's school. The mentoring program coordinator may be able to help by scheduling afterschool mentoring time at a centralized location.

Mentor and Mentee Personalities Clash

This is a tough situation. Mentors have to remain professional in their work with mentees. You know you have made a commitment and that, sometimes, honoring commitments becomes very difficult. Keeping the goals of the mentoring program in mind, the mentor's reaction to the mentee has to be above reproach. The mentor needs to remain professional no matter how petty the interactions with the mentee may become, because less professional responses would undermine the program goals. The mentoring program coordinator may need to arbitrate. This issue is much too delicate to leave unattended. Clear communication between the mentor and mentoring program coordinator could save the relationship.

Mentee Is Asking Too Much of the Mentor

The mentee may see the mentor-mentee relationship as a *great* thing. This is a way to get help on demand. He or she could take the demands too far. The mentor's role is to *support*—not *save*—the mentee. It's not too far a stretch to believe that any teacher may exhibit a classic case of learned helplessness when faced with the demands of a classroom of twenty-four special needs students. The mentor should return to the mentee needs assessment and the action plan and review with the mentee what goals they have set and how they are going to accomplish these goals. Be clear with the mentee that the roles and responsibilities of a mentor do not permit the mentor to *do* the mentee's work or be available on demand. Again, this is an instance where the mentoring program coordinator may need to arbitrate.

WHAT DO MENTORS GAIN FROM THE EXPERIENCE?

With the increased interest in retention and the widespread use of mentoring programs as a way to socialize as well as retain new teachers, mentor programs are becoming more common. Some mentoring programs include ways to recognize or even pay the mentors for their work. Some mentoring projects include a reassignment of duties to allow mentors to work with new teachers without cost to their own classroom teaching. That may be the ideal situation, and not replicable across the country. Mentor programs that do not come with built-in remuneration have other ways to validate the service mentors give to the profession.

Professional Development. Railsback and Brewster (2001) provide numerous advantages to mentors for participation in mentoring programs. First, mentors are able to spend time in different classrooms. To professional teachers, this is a way to continue their own professional improvement. We always learn from what we see others doing—sometimes we learn new, better tactics; sometimes we learn what we will never do.

Second, mentoring enables mentors to build a living theory of teaching out of practice. The mentors and mentees can develop a philosophy of how to teach their students at their school. This is not written down in any text; rather, it is lived and learned on the job.

Collegiality. Third, mentoring increases the skills teachers need to work with adults in a collegial, collaborative manner. The communication and collaboration skills in Chapter 5 and the adult learning skills described in Chapter 6 will be used to further the interpersonal relationships established between mentors and mentees and they will be equally as useful beyond the mentoring relationship.

Recognition of Service and Skills. Fourth, the mentoring process provides professional teachers the chance to rejuvenate themselves by sharing in the success of other teachers. The recognition he or she should receive as a master teacher and mentor adds "pizzazz" to the routines of teaching.

Last, the mentoring process encourages participation in professional networks of other mentors and encourages sharing. If a mentoring program is done correctly, the mentors as well as the mentees receive ongoing support. The ongoing support of the mentors can include contact with other mentors to hear success stories and describe challenges. Even in school districts where staff development monies are cut "to the bone," their peers and administrators can tout the rewards of mentoring in the way these master teachers are recognized.

WHAT IF?

You were asked by the special education director to become a mentor for new special education teachers in your district. Your school system is located in a rural area of the state and schools are several miles apart. You know that you'll have to drive a significant distance to get to your mentee's school. This plays a big part in your answer to becoming a mentor. You are also unsure of how the time away from your school will be evaluated by your principal. How do you respond?

Possible Responses Include the Following:

Discuss the value of mentoring with your principal and see how he or she feels about your time away from school.

Visit the mentee's school and determine whether online mentoring is possible for some of the needed support.

Help the mentee identify an onsite mentor who can socialize the mentee to the school's politics while you help socialize the mentee to special education politics.

REFERENCES

Brewster, C., & Railsback, J. (2001). *Supporting beginning teachers: How administrators, teachers and policymakers can help new teachers succeed.* Portland, OR: Northwest Regional Educational Laboratory. Retrieved September 1, 2003, from http://www .nwrel.org/request/may01/index.html

Cheney, C. O., Krajewski, J., & Combs, M. (1992). Understanding the first year teacher: Implications for induction programs. *Teacher Education and Special Education, 15*(1), 18–24.

Moir, E. (1999). The stages of a teacher's first year. In M. Scherer (Ed.), *A better beginning: Supporting and mentoring new teachers* (pp. 19–23). Alexandria, VA: ASCD.

Richardson, V., Anders, P., Tidwell, D., & Lloyd, C. (1991). The relationship between teachers' beliefs and practices in reading comprehension. *American Educational Research Journal, 28,* 559–586.

Rowley, J. B. (1999). The good mentor. *Educational Leadership, 56*(8), 20–22.

Whitaker, S. D. (2003). Needs of beginning special education teachers: Implications for teacher education. *Teacher Education and Special Education, 26*(2), 106–117.

Effective Communication Skills 5

VIGNETTE

Mr. Jones has been very helpful as a friend lending an occasional ear. This has been vital for me because friendships are important to me. He has listened when I really did not need to hear anything but my own voice. He also likes his voice and fortunately has offered wonderful advice.

—Beth Merritt

 95

Mentors are coaches. Mentors are gurus. Mentors are sounding boards. They have so many roles and all of them rely on the mentor's ability to communicate. Effective communication skills are crucial to any mentoring relationship. We will spend a great deal of time talking about the communication skills needed to facilitate a positive mentoring relationship. National Public Radio's *Talk of the Nation* (Pugnaire & Hall, 2003) featured a story about the latest trend in medical school practices. Doctors are now being trained to listen and communicate more effectively with their patients. They are given mock patients to interview and practice effective interpersonal communication skills (we used to call it bedside manner). When the speaker was asked about why doctors need to learn these skills, she stated that communication skills were central to quality medical care. The interviewer was incredulous that doctors did not already know how to speak to patients. Every professional needs to pay more attention to how they communicate, doctors and mentors included.

EFFECTIVE COMMUNICATION SKILLS

An effective mentor needs effective communication skills to keep the relationship going. The essential communication skills needed by a mentor include those that allow the mentor to listen actively, yet not judgmentally, and those that allow them to express ideas clearly. Those skills include nonverbal communication, negotiation, and encouragement.

Listening. The short poem that follows captures the essence of effective listening without having to read too deeply. Sometimes when a person has to talk with you they do not need to be "fixed." Rather, they just need to be listened to; a simple rule to be considered when working with new and veteran teachers alike.

On Listening

When I ask you to listen to me and you start
giving me advice, you have not done what I asked.

When I ask you to listen to me and you begin to tell me

why I shouldn't feel that way, you are trampling on my feelings.

When I ask you to listen to me and you feel you have

to do something to solve my problems,
you have failed me, strange as that may seem.

Listen! All I ask is that you listen.

Not talk or do—just hear me.

When you do something for me that
I can and need to do for myself, you contribute
to my fear and inadequacy.

And I can do for my self. I'm not helpless;
maybe discouraged and faltering, but not helpless.

So please, listen and just hear me.

And, if you want to talk, wait a minute
for your turn, I'll listen to you.

—Author unknown

Listening is a crucial skill for mentors. It is not an easy task to be a good listener. Many things interfere with a person's ability to listen effectively. Rehearsing a response, daydreaming, stumbling over controversial words or ideas, filtering messages, and being distracted by the details are just a few of these things. If a listener is constantly jumping for a chance to talk/respond, they may miss the intent of the message or the hidden message in the conversation. Likewise, avoiding or fixating on hot topics or controversial words may mask the real message being sent. Of all the distractions, the one that can cause the most problems is the filtering of messages. What this refers to is the listener's ability to turn off the message because he or she does not have a frame of reference for the conversation, or has an overfamiliarity with the topic. For example, the new special education teacher wants to go back over the process for IEP meetings. In your mind this is a simple process! It was discussed thoroughly at a recent special education meeting. You don't want to hear about it any more—or talk about it any more. So you tune out. That's filtering. Or you are talking with someone who is sharing information that you know nothing about—you tune out because you can't make the connection to what they are sharing. That's filtering. This is a troublesome distraction in that, if the speaker perceives that you have tuned out, he or she also perceives that what he or she has to say doesn't have value. In a mentoring relationship this does more harm than expected.

There are physical and emotional barriers to effective listening. When you are reading this list, think about whether they are physical or emotional barriers and what you might do to counteract or overcome these barriers.

- I'm hungry.

- I already know this.

- I don't care.

- I have a headache.

- I can't hear.

- I'm tired.

- I'm not responsible for this information.

- I don't understand.

- I'm bored.

- This doesn't relate to me.

- There is spinach in her teeth!

- People around me are talking.

- Did she say *inclusion?*

- What should my answer be?

- What should I buy for tonight's dinner?

- This isn't even feasible.

Some of these responses are the result of not being motivated or not feeling part of the process. Some are the result of not having enough information to build a connection. Some are just notions that make a fleeting appearance in our consciousness, just long enough to pull us away from the task. The effective speaker has to consider how the message is being received before it's even been sent. The effective speaker has to consider the capacity of the listeners to listen before sending the message. Within the mentoring relationship the mentor has to consciously attune to the mentee's comments and questions. The mentor's role is to listen and encourage interaction between the mentoring pair.

Verbal and Nonverbal Communication. Listening is only one-half of the communication process. The other half is made up of our abilities to use language effectively, both verbal and nonverbal language. Verbal communication is the give-and-take of conversation between two people. For a mentor, communication skills can be characterized as a democratic, human resources style more so than other types of communication. That means that the mode of communication is collegial, collaborative, ethical, and skillful (Far West Labs, 1990).

This communication thing is not really that easy. It's not usually a one-way street. Usually the act of communicating is more than just speaking or listening. The speaker considers the listener and vice versa.

An excellent example of how communication works is to participate in a *triad* activity. In this activity the leader breaks a larger group into smaller groups of three. Within each group of three, identify a listener, speaker, and observer. The speaker talks about a topic of his or her choosing for three minutes. The listener must listen without giving any feedback for the entire three minutes. That means no head nods, no "hmmms," and no questions. The listener just sits and listens for three minutes. The observer watches the body language of the speaker and listener and observes speech patterns, conversation patterns (how many "you knows?" in a sentence, etc.). At the end of the three minutes the speaker is relieved to be finished talking— "Longest three minutes in my life!" And the listener is just jumping at the chance to add something to the conversation. Sometimes the observer is drawn into the conversation because the speaker cannot get any feedback from the listener, so he or she starts speaking to the observer. The observer typically sees the listener showing nonverbal signs of defense—arms crossed, sitting straight in chair. That usually means the listener is exhibiting extra restraint different from his or her usual response to the situation.

A good mentor is able to gauge when to listen and when to interject commentary. For example, consider the outcome of an interchange between a mentor and a mentee prior to an eligibility meeting, the first the mentee is to attend. The mentee may have a few questions about process that are easily answered by the mentor. The mentor, on the other hand, carefully listens to see whether the mentee is focused only on their role or the mentee is looking outward to understand how the whole meeting will be run. If the mentee is inwardly focused, the mentor can ask probing questions to refocus the mentee perception (How will you draw out the parent in the meeting? What should the general education teachers bring with them?, etc.). If the mentee is already asking questions to indicate that he or she is thinking about the overall meeting, the mentor can reinforce this perception and support the mentee's plans for the meeting.

What does all this mean? *Communication is rarely unilateral.* Rarely do people speak to themselves. Even the chefs on TV have an in-studio audience to and with which to talk. We encounter unilateral communication most frequently when we send e-mail or regular mail. This type of communication is to be read without an audience reacting instantaneously in our presence. That's not to say that we sometimes do react instantaneously when we read an e-mail that touches a chord.

Communication is often directive. We as teachers are very good at directive communication. We tell students how to do things, how to behave. We even try the same type of communication with adults (our spouses) and that type of communication is not as effective in those adult-to-adult situations.

Communication is transactional. Communication is most often meant to be interacted with. The speaker intends the listener to give verbal and nonverbal feedback.

Barriers that both speakers and listeners set up impede the effectiveness of communication. In 1970, Thomas Gordon wrote about the barriers to communication that can be applied to the mentor-mentee relationship. He described the 12 barriers as blocking rather than promoting communication. India Podsen and Vicki Denmark (2000) took Gordon's idea one step further to describe the barrier in terms of the effects they have on the listener. First, let's look at Gordon's Barriers to communication and then we'll consider Podsen and Denmark's comments on the effect on communication between mentor and mentee the barriers may present (see Table 5.1).

It is obvious that most mentors would not respond in the ways captured in the chart above. But don't let that divert your focus from the real barriers that are present in communication. A mentor may not threaten a mentee in exactly the same way as the chart indicates, but may choose a more subtle statement like "Doing that could be a real problem for you down the road." The intent is similar; the mentor is warning the mentee that trouble could be ahead if you do not do it "my way." The mentor may be exactly right—there could be problems; however, the presentation style is what turns this statement of advice into a potential barrier. Consider how it would sound if instead of offering a warning the mentor offered to talk about the wider perspective. How choices fit or do not fit into the bigger picture of the school. Then the threat or warning is seen as advice.

Table 5.1   Thomas Gordon's barriers to communication

Barrier	Description	Example
Criticizing	Making a negative evaluation of the novice	"You've brought this on yourself—you've got no one else to blame."
Name calling	Putting down or stereotyping the novice	"All beginners are just alike."
Diagnosing	Analyzing why the novice is behaving as he or she is; playing amateur psychiatrist	"Just because you have had courses on a more current curriculum in college doesn't mean you know what is best."
Praising evaluatively	Making a positive judgment about the novice	"You're the perfect role model."
Ordering	Commanding the person to do what you want to have done	"I want those bulletin boards changed tomorrow."
Threatening	Trying to control the novice's actions by warning of a negative consequence	"Attend the PTO meeting tonight or I'll report this to your supervisor."
Moralizing	Tell the novice what he should do; preaching	"You should cut your hair—it's too long."
Excessive questioning	Asking closed questions	"Did you spend much time on your lesson plans?"
Advising	Giving the novice a solution to his or her problem	"If I were you, I'd tell the parents. . . ."
Diverting	Pushing the novice's problems aside through distraction	"You think you're tired? Let me tell you about when I was. . . ."
Logical argument	Attempting to convince the novice with an appeal to facts or logic without consideration of the emotional factors involved	"Look at the facts. If you hadn't been absent yesterday, the unit would be completed."
Reassuring	Trying to stop the other person from feeling the negative emotions he or she is experiencing	"Don't worry about that lesson. You will still pass the course."

SOURCE: Adapted from Podsen and Denmark (2000, pp. 50–51).

The same idea can be used to break down other barriers as well. Negative evaluation comments can be couched as feedback. It is more than just semantics; it is making sure the listener understands the basis for the comments. Making sure the listener understands the frame of reference.

Encouraging. The mentor is most often the cheerleader for the mentee. The mentor rejoices with the mentee when things are going well and bolsters the mentee when problems loom. Caccia (1999) describes one concept, "Linguistic Coaching," as one technique that inspires and encourages new teachers. Linguistic coaching is based on the idea that "speaking and listening can be categorized as some sort of action—stating, promising, requesting, asserting, declaring, replying—in which the speaker makes a commitment with the listener" (p. 158). When a mentor and mentee talk about the daily events, they use verbs to describe the day's events. "My students didn't *get* the lesson I *tried* to present on fractions. When I *asked* them a question, they just *looked* at me blankly." The mentor and mentee would look at the actions taking place and frame them with respect to how they could be interpreted. Were the students not getting it because I was unclear? Were they not getting it because I went too quickly? Did they look blankly because they didn't understand? Did they not answer because they don't like to guess? The encouraging statements made by the mentor would be based on the interpretations of the events.

A note of caution: The interpretations may vary from a shared reality because of frame of reference. For example, culture, experiences, or emotions may color the interpretation one could make. If the mentor's and mentee's interpretations are in opposition, the mentor will not make the desired connection with the mentee. The suggestions will be lost or unheeded. Clarity of the shared perceptions is crucial. The mentor can make the most difference by encouraging a mentee when both know that the encouragement will lead to a commonly held value or goal. For example, if you tell me that new special education teachers typically have a great deal of trouble getting organized and you've observed my skill at organization, then your observation about my skill in organization is appreciated—it encourages me to go on, to get better. However, if I don't know that organization is a big hurdle for many new teachers, then I don't understand why you keep telling me I'm doing a good job at organizing the lesson. Was that the only thing I did right?

OBSERVING AND COACHING

Assessment Through Observation. An article by Shui-fong Lam (1999) described teachers' perceptions regarding the usefulness of observation as a staff development tool. She reported that special educators and secondary-level teachers are the most welcoming of observers and observer comments. The study went on to describe the value of having someone watch others teach as a way to learn how to improve their own teaching. Again, the special education teachers surveyed indicated that they benefited from this type of staff development. This is great news for mentors, because mentors often have their mentees observe them, and they in turn observe the mentees as part of the socialization process.

Objectivity in Observing. One technique, used to organize observational feedback is through a technique called "360-degree feedback." Karen Dyer (2001) translated Fleenor and Prince's (1997) description of how 360-degree feedback works by focusing on these essential characteristics of the process:

- Feedback is formative, not summative

- Mentoring is part of the feedback follow-up

- An action plan is developed directly from the results of the formative observations

- The entire process is confidential

Giving Constructive Feedback. Each element of 360-degree observation sounds very much like a mentoring relationship. And in many ways it is. Mentors provide building blocks for improvement within the context of their feedback. Their feedback is always formative. Mentors do not provide evaluative feedback; they are not called on to give feedback to anyone regarding the effectiveness of the mentees' instruction. Mentors do not evaluate their mentees' practice. Mentors work along with the mentees to develop new skills and refine existing ones. The mentor role is not one of an expert directing a novice on how to complete a task. The mentor works *with* the mentee. Effective mentor-mentee relationships are based on plans that document the goals the team is working toward. These goals are easily seen as action plans. And of course, the mentor-mentee relationship is always confidential.

TEAMING: WORKING
WITH OTHERS EFFECTIVELY

In special education, we talk about consultants who provide services to help teachers and parents efficiently work with students. These consultants use a very specific form of communication skills. They consult. Sometimes we talk about teachers collaborating to solve problems. They too use a specific form of communication: collaboration. There is a difference between the two. The context of the interaction should determine whether you use collaborative or consultative interactions. Knowing when to use which style of communication is the key issue. By understanding what collaboration and consultation means, you can make better choices.

Collaboration, Consultation, and Teaming. The participants in a collaborative interchange have to place the same degree of importance on the issue. You cannot force anyone to be collaborative. You cannot force anyone to solve problems collaboratively or share in the responsibility or accountability of a collaborative decision. This does not mean that issues that come from outside (mandated programs, initiatives that come from the top down, etc.) cannot be solved collaboratively; rather, the goals become the collaborative connection.

Collaboration is based on mutual goals. If a general education teacher and a special education teacher are members of a seventh-grade team, they already have a common goal—the seventh graders they teach. Everything they do can be couched in terms of the common goal. So while the membership of the team may not be voluntary, the goals they work toward can be mutually developed.

Barriers to Effective Collaboration. If one person on a team is seen as having more power (which could in some cases be translated into more expertise), then collaboration is harder to obtain. A team could be diligently working toward the shared goal, but if one of the team members has the final say in the decision-making process, then the collaborative process is severely hampered. The Teacher Assistance Team (TAT) model (Chalfant, Pysch, & Moultrie, 1979) is a school-based support model that makes use of teacher expertise to solve instructional and behavioral classroom problems. The research Chalfant and Pysch carried out during the late 1980s indicated that these school-based teams had greater success in helping general classroom teachers solve their own problems when the special education teacher, administrator, or school psychologist did not participate in the problem-solving sessions. Follow-up interviews indicated that the teachers on the teams would look toward the special education teacher to come up with the "right answer" and not generate any other options when they were part of the TAT. When an administrator served on the team, issues of evaluation entered into the problem-solving process. Pairs of teachers working together seemed to have greater success in meeting student needs and in developing collegial relationships that lasted beyond the team meetings.

Professionals who collaborate trust one another. Teachers are often hesitant to discuss their failures in front of the principal for fear that evaluation would enter into the problem-solving process. School psychologists are sometimes seen as outsiders to the classroom and their input is discounted as not necessarily appropriate for the classroom. These teacher responses underscore how important parity is to collaborative interchanges.

Team Processes. Teachers who develop a solution to a problem share responsibility for the delivery of the service and the outcomes obtained. The degree to which this is done is a measure of the level of commitment the individual has in solving the problem. Imagine how an IEP meeting might change if the information shared by the parties present (parents, psychologist, teachers) becomes the basis for the student's program, and that program is then delivered by the team who generated the ideas. Not just by the teacher in the classroom. Would the teachers be quick to blame the parents (and vice versa) if they knew that what was needed for this child to succeed is being carried out by all the parties involved; that everyone has their role and can be counted on to meet the commitment? This type of relationship between the members of a problem-solving team fosters interdependence. *A sense of community evolves from collaboration.*

Here's the bottom line: collaboration and consultation will work in a school if, and only if, the people involved are prepared for the roles, understand their specific roles, and know the goals for the process. The new special education teacher needs to know whom to depend on for role-specific advice. Let's go back to the example of a new special education teacher who has two mentors. One is the on-site mentor who does not teach special education. The mentee can rely on the on-site mentor for general information about how the school and district works, what curricula are available to all students, and so forth. The second mentor is one that has specific knowledge of special education processes and policies.

A cautionary note: It is crucial that the mentors do not try to answer questions clearly in the expertise of the other mentor—the confusing information will not help the mentee.

PROBLEM SOLVING

In most cases the mentor and mentee have convivial, supportive relationships, but we are dealing with people. Disagreements do arise and problems have to be addressed. To begin a discussion on problem solving we have to know whether the situation allows us to be proactive or reactive. This is an important distinction to make. The way one will approach a problem will be vastly different if one can see the problem in the offing, as opposed to those problems that blindside the individual. Problems that have a limited reaction time require more direct action where problems in the offing allow one to collaborate and seek help from beyond the immediate circle of support. Remember, time was also integral to collaboration. Crisis or short-term encounters are usually best solved using a consultative method.

Your own personal problem-solving techniques change with each situation. As the situation changes, so do your preferences. The emotional attachment would cause you to look at the problem in a different way than if you were using a cool, clear, objective lens. If you are able to employ more techniques, you still need to keep in mind the context for each style of resolution.

1. *Competitive or forced resolution* is used when a solution is needed immediately or the possibility of not having a solution is disastrous.

2. *Collaborative problem solving* is used when the relationship between the two parties is seen as a long-term relationship. The two parties are anticipating working together now and in the future. This takes into account the idea of time.

3. *Compromising* is used when the individual parties can find ways to give up something to make the overall plan work. Compromise is useful when the two parties are invested in the solution or outcome.

4. *Avoiding* could be seen as a negative technique, but in some cases it is a preferred technique that will allow the individuals to obtain information that may be helpful to the overall solution. Or one party needs to obtain outside support in order to solve the problem. Avoiding becomes negative when the situation is never resolved.

5. *Accommodating or smoothing* is a technique that is useful when the two parties appear very far apart. This technique allows the mediator to look for a similarity (or similarities) to build a compromise upon. Accommodation allows the parties to highlight the ways they agree rather than accentuating the ways they vary.

Supportive Release. There is one specific element of problem solving that is important to the mentoring relationship that may not be part of other team problem-solving relationships. When a mentor and protégé discuss options or solutions, the mentor has to know when to step back and allow the mentee to try solving the problem without help. This is called supportive release. The mentor and mentee can talk through the process, discuss pitfalls, and rehearse outcomes, but the mentor has to stop short of actually solving the problem for the mentee to become an independent problem solver. Special educators are very familiar with this type of technique. They use it with students who are learning to be independent in decision-making. The same is true for mentors and mentees. The mentor has to let the mentee try his or her wings. Kindler's resource on *Managing Disagreements Constructively* (1988) also identifies supportive release as a viable solution for conflict. Kindler chooses to employ this technique when the two problem solvers cannot come to consensus and one participant in the problem-solving scenario chooses to support the decision of the other member. However, in an educational setting the mentor chooses to support the mentee's efforts at solving a problem independently. This allows a boost in confidence for the mentee and less dependence on the mentor's skills.

WHAT IF?

Every time you visit with your mentee you feel welcome and a part of the mentee's class. However, when you sit down to debrief or talk about what went on that day, the mentee's eyes glaze over. You realize that this has been happening more frequently when you get together. This person never turned you away or rejected your help. What can you do to help the communication situation?

Possible Solutions

1. We use dialogue journals with students all the time. Maybe a dialogue journal or an e-mail dialogue will help with the glazed-over stares. The mentee may need time to think and reflect beyond the classroom. Dialoguing online or on paper may provide that think time.

2. Check to see if the mentee is struggling with the daily and weekly workload. Maybe time management is needed and the individual does not know how to ask for that sort of help.

REFERENCES

Brubaker, D. L., & Simon, L. H. (1993). *Teacher as decision maker: Real-life cases to hone your people skills.* Newbury Park, CA: Corwin Press.

Caccia, P. (1999). Linguistic coaching: Helping beginning teachers defeat discouragement. In M. Scherer (Ed.), *A better beginning: Supporting and mentoring new teachers.* Alexandria, VA: ASCD.

Chalfant, J., Pysch, M., & Moultrie, R. (1979). Teacher assistance teams: A model for within-building problem solving. *Learning Disability Quarterly, 2*(3), 85–96.

Cramer, S. F. (1998). *Collaboration: A success strategy for special educators.* Boston: Allyn & Bacon.

Dyer, K. M. (2001). The power of 360-degree feedback. *Educational Leadership, 58*(5), 35–38.

Fleenor, J. W., & Prince, J. M. (1997). *Using 360-degree feedback in organizations: An annotated bibliography.* Greensboro, NC: Center for Creative Leadership.

Gordon, T. (1970). *Parent effectiveness training: The no-lose program for training responsible children.* New York: Peter Wyden.

Jonson, K. F. (2002). *Being an effective mentor: How to help beginning teachers to succeed.* Thousand Oaks, CA: Corwin Press.

Kindler, H. S. (1988). *Managing disagreement constructively: A practical guide for constructive conflict management.* Los Altos, CA: Crisp.

Lam, Shui-fong. (1999). Educators' opinion on classroom observation as a practice of staff development and appraisal. *Teaching and Teacher Education, 17*(2), 161–173.

Little, J. W., & Nelson, L. (Eds.). (1990). *A leader's guide to mentor training.* San Francisco: Far West Regional Laboratory for Education Research and Development.

Podsen, I. J., & Denmark, V. M. (2000). *Coaching and mentoring first-year and student teachers.* Larchmont, NY: Eye on Education.

Pugnaire, M., & Hall, T. (Interviewees). (2003). *Doctor-patient communication.* [Internet audio archive of National Public Radio: Talk of the Nation]. Retrieved on July 29, 2004, from http://www.npr.org/features/feature.php?wfId=1344267

Here are some online resources for communication skill development:

- http://www.see.ed.ac.uk/~gerard/Management/art7.html

The second site is an article from the business world that relates communication skills to specific events (e.g., meetings). The benefit of this article is that it provides an out-of-school look at communication. It's one of those frame of reference things again. If the person you are talking to takes a business world approach, then you ought to respond in a business world manner. This will provide you with some tools beyond education material.

- http://www.worldhelloday.org/

Just for fun. Mark this one on your calendars!

- http://www.manifestation.com/neurotoys/calibrate.php3

A long time ago I heard some speakers talking about how to make communication more effective if you watch the speaker's eyes and track their movement as they talk or think. This was done by a group of folks who studied Neurolinguistic Programming (NLP). This Web site is included for you to see yet another way to think about communication. If you search the Internet for NLP world you'll get even more stuff on that information base.

- http://www.creatingstrategies.com/virtual_coach/coaching_gym/communication_coaching

This next site is a virtual communication skills coach. You can access the site and have the virtual coach help you figure out what elements of communication you are good at and where you might need help. You can also get a virtual coach for your spiritual life! Not that a mentor might need that one!

Learning About Adult Learners 6

VIGNETTE

My sense is that the mentoring of adults (which I had not thought of until one of my doctoral students announced in a public forum that her mentor, me!, was in the audience) is somewhat of an innate, automatic response. Have you ever stopped someone who looked bewildered and said, "You look lost. Can I help you?" It is much like that. It is knowing when/where/why/how to ask a question, to listen, to offer unasked for advice (and when not to), to offer a collaborative opportunity, to offer an opportunity that could enhance your career but would enhance someone else's career even more, and to ask for help yourself (and that takes some self-grounding, guts, and trust!). While some personalities "click" easier and some professional backgrounds bond easier, someone who mentors overlooks the differences that can separate and focuses on what will make someone else successful.

—Elliott Lessen

WORKING WITH ADULTS

It is commonly held that adults learn differently from children and even from adolescents. The study of how adults learn, sometimes called andragogy, was promulgated by Malcolm Knowles and his associates in 1984. In this chapter, we will discuss the tenets of andragogy and their connection to mentoring new special education teachers as a foundation to the discussion of the mentoring process. Mentoring relationships will succeed at a greater rate if mentors are aware of the difference in the way adults learn. Mentors are all accomplished teachers *of children or adolescents,* but not every mentor is an accomplished teacher of adults. Good teachers understand what they have to do to get students to learn. They are often direct in their interactions, and use directive statements for the students to follow. New teachers need less direction and more confidence building as part of their learning style. Mentors who relate to their mentee as they would their students may not maximize the mentor-mentee relationship (Fawcett, 1997).

Specific Needs of Adult Learners. Adults need differing contexts and practices to learn new ideas and concepts. Just as adolescent learners need autonomy and structure to learn effectively, the adult learner also learns best when specific conditions are present. Jane Vella (2002) has built on Knowles' (1984) idea of adult learning theory to delimit the conditions necessary for adult learning to take place. Her research has identified 12 principles for effective adult learning. These principles should become key elements of techniques mentors use when working with a new special education teacher.

Adult Learning Theory and Motivation

Vella's Twelve Principles for Effective Adult Learning

- *Needs assessment:* participation of the learners in naming what is to be learned.
- *Safety* in the environment and the process. We create a context for learning. That context can be made safe.
- *Sound relationships* between teacher and learner and among learners.
- *Sequence* of content and *reinforcement.*
- *Praxis:* action with reflection or learning by doing.
- *Respect for learners as decision makers.*
- *Ideas, feeling, and actions:* cognitive, affective, and psychomotor aspects of learning.
- *Immediacy* of the learning.
- *Clear roles and role development.*
- *Teamwork* and use of small groups.
- *Engagement* of the learners in what they are learning.
- *Accountability:* how do they know they know?

SOURCE: Vella, 2002, p. 4

Let us look at each element of effective adult learning and identify its observable components. Later in the chapter, we will look at how adult learning needs apply to a special education mentorship.

Needs Assessment

Before a learning experience is designed for an adult population, a needs assessment is conducted. In her book, Vella is very specific about the key questions used in a needs assessment. She focuses on the "WWW questions . . . who as needers, what as needs, and whom as definers" (p. 5). She goes on to explain that professionals who work with adult learners need to present new information in a context that explains who needs the new information, what is needed to accomplish the new task, and who defines the new task or skill. The need for innovation to occur in this context is clear when one recalls the theories on adult learning presented by Knowles. Adults are more motivated to learn when they are part of the process, and the new learning directly makes their situation better. Therefore, when a mentor and mentee are designing a plan of action for the year, the mentor has to take the following into account:

1. *Who is the mentee?* Is the mentee new to the district? Is the mentee new to teaching? Is the mentee new to the grade level? All three categories indicate different needs that an individual may have.

2. *What needs does the mentee present?* Has this person taught in a self-contained program before? Is this person experienced in working with individuals with autism?

3. *Who is defining the mentee's needs?* Are there school-specific constraints that factor in? Is the principal special-education friendly? Are there expectations within the community that play a part in the way the school is run?

The needs assessment looks at the defining attributes of the person, the place, and the tasks associated with the mentee's job. The mentor and mentee generate a yearly action plan related to this assessment. Action planning is discussed fully in Chapter 3.

Safety

The key to a successful mentoring relationship is the development of trust. A sense of safety is borne out of trust. Adults enter new learning situations with prior knowledge. Sometimes the prior knowledge includes instances when trust was violated, causing future relationships to be entered into cautiously.

Special education mentors can build trust between themselves and their mentees by first making their competence clear. Assure mentees through conversation and observation that mentors understand the "new teacher" situation. Also assure mentees that mentors have the desire and skills to help. Another way mentors can build trust and safety is to explain the mentoring process by defining roles and rules. Explain that you, as a mentor, are a support and not an evaluator. Describe how the school's mentoring program will help new teachers, not put more responsibilities on them. A third way to build trust and safety is to encourage mentees to attend new teacher meetings. During this experience, the new special education teacher sees that what they are experiencing is not unique. They will also hear about other mentor-mentee relationships and realize that others are seeing mentors as helpful, not as a hindrance. The last way mentors can build trust and safety is to understand that the process of opening up is gradual. A mentee is not expected to confide every anxiety or concern to a mentor during the first week of school. The mentor continually builds trust with the mentee by being consistent in behavior (e.g., offering support, giving reality-based feedback, setting up small attainable goals).

Sound Relationships

Jane Vella uses the sound relationship principle as a way to talk about investment. As the special education mentor-mentee relationships begin, mentors should engage mentees in a discussion about what they want to get out of the mentoring process. Vella indicated in her book that this discussion should take place early in the relationship and ideally during the action planning process. However, action planning can occur informally via e-mail or small group discussion sessions where several new special education teachers get together at the beginning of the year.

One caveat offered by Vella is that the discussion must "transcend personal likes and dislikes and obvious differences in power" (p. 11). That is to say that the mentor has to listen openly to the mentee's requests, not belittling or overestimating them. Mentors and mentees should remember that their primary goal is to help students learn and that individual differences regarding clothing, friends, diets, and so forth should not hinder the mentoring process.

Sequence and Reinforcement

The principles of sequence and reinforcement are basic tenets of special education practice. If you want to learn something new, first sequence the task from simple to complex or from concrete to abstract and then teach it that way. Follow the instruction with plenty of opportunities for reinforcement. Sequence and reinforcement are also part of the adult learning process.

Consider how school district personnel present a new instructional curriculum to teachers. The staff development personnel might indicate that the old curriculum had its strong points, but that this new curriculum is much better. For instance, the new curriculum contains more research-validated practices, more critical thinking questions, and Web site addresses for enriched learning. The curriculum is presented as a new and better method for teaching. The staff developers highlight the similarities with the older curriculum and then move into the things that make the new curriculum even better: that is sequencing. If you are mentoring a new special education teacher, the sequence builds on what he or she already knows. The opportunities for reinforcement are structured so that one new skill is mastered before another is introduced.

Praxis

The idea of praxis is really part of an observation cycle. When an evaluator observes a teacher, the ideal situation would include a debriefing meeting afterward to talk about the quality of the instruction. Of course, in a mentoring situation evaluation is not the goal of observation. When a mentor watches the special education mentee teach, the debriefing conference is focused on what the *mentee* perceives they did well or what needs work. The debriefing conference serves as a guided reflection activity. The mentor asks open-ended questions to help the mentee reflect. What was successful? How does one know that was successful? What goals were attained? How does one know those goals were attained? Where does one go from here? What needs attention?

The intent is to help the novice learn to be self-evaluative, as praxis is an ongoing process that does not end when tenure is achieved. This is not an easy task. Some mentees are resistant to revealing faults or hesitant to name goals for improvement. A technique that may help is simulated recall. This technique is sometimes used in qualitative research to help the subject reflect on an episode.

Fifty years ago, Benjamin Bloom (1953) described stimulated recall as a method to retrieve the memories of students after a class, a way to help them recall their thoughts. The use of a videotaped teaching segment and a debriefing conference, where the mentor asks self-evaluative questions of the mentee, is one way to apply the stimulated recall concept to mentoring. A cautionary note: Many people feel uncomfortable seeing themselves on television, so beginning with an audiotape reflection may be less threatening.

Respect for Learners as Decision Makers

Adults are decision makers in most areas of their lives. Teachers make decisions for numerous other individuals in a split second. Veteran teachers are extremely experienced at making decisions. The special education mentee has to learn this skill and practice as part of the mentoring relationship. The mentor does help the mentee by making decisions for them. Rather, the mentor should offer options and help the mentee think through the choices, leaving the decision up to the mentee. If the mentee is a traditional-age new special education teacher (23–25 years old), then the mentor may have to be more specific in comparing the options, but the mentor cannot make the decision for the mentee even if the mentee is 23 years old.

Ideas, Feelings, Actions

The adult learner uses mind, heart, and body to learn new concepts and skills. Think about learning to use a new e-mail tool. The manual may help, but if you have someone sit with you and show you how to retrieve e-mail, respond to e-mail, and add an attachment, the process does not seem as mystifying. The same is true with a new IEP form. Most districts provide new special education teachers training in writing the compliance points of an IEP. The forms seem easy during the training but the new special education teacher may become challenged when writing one independently. Having a mentor help you write the first few IEPs is far superior to referring to workshop handouts alone.

The appreciation of ideas, feelings, and actions can be used to lessen fear related to a new activity. Talking about an upcoming evaluation by the principal can be less traumatic if the mentor describes what will happen from a cognitive, an affective, and a psychomotor perspective. This briefing helps the new special education teacher teach the observation with confidence because she knows the expectations.

Immediacy

Adult learners desire immediacy of results. They are willing to break a task down into smaller elements as long as progress can be measured in completing the elements on the way to completing the whole task. Successes along the way encourage learners to continue and complete the task. This process allows mentors to provide feedback along the way, and not delay it until the end of projects.

Another characteristic of immediacy is the idea that smaller chunks are better than one big chunk. Workshops or inservice activities are more effective when delivered in smaller units with a variety of ways of reporting or measuring progress. In a mentoring relationship, this means frequent short meetings with your mentee are more useful than day-long work sessions.

Clear Roles

In a mentoring relationship, several ground rules have to be established before the mentor and mentee can work together. First, the mentor is not there to evaluate. The mentee should expect confidentiality in conversations with the mentor. Second, the mentor was selected because of a desire to mentor a new special education teacher. Becoming a mentor was a choice. Third, the goal of mentoring is to help the new teacher adjust to a new school, new class, and new job. In the mentoring relationship, the mentee's needs are foremost. Last, the mentor is a veteran teacher, but is not the mentee's superior. They are coworkers and colleagues working toward a common goal.

It is crucial that the mentor and mentee discuss the ground rules and concepts before they begin. The pair may also want to talk about very basic ground rules, like what to call each other, whether borrowing each other's material is acceptable, whether calling each other at home is proper, and so on. By engaging in a discussion of rules, the channels of communication are opened rather than limited.

Teamwork

The mentoring pair is really a team. While teaming in school is most often represented in the process that special educators use to determine eligibility, develop and maintain educational plans and programs, and solve problems, teaming is also used in many new teacher programs to support new teachers in a specific department or area (e.g., special education, fourth-grade teachers). The skills needed for effective teaming are the cornerstone of collaboration. The following are required for an effective team:

- Awareness of team membership: simply stated, this means you are part of the team. You have the *official* team shirt!

- Shared norms govern interactions: Everyone is there because they have the same goal in mind. This does not mean ground rules are discarded. The ground rules set parameters on the patterns of communication. Consider how differently a team will speak when a student is present versus times when the student is not there. Those are the unstated ground rules.

- Team members are interdependent; the group makes decisions. Everyone is part of the decision. Each member owns the outcome.

- Team members have unique skills and perspectives: Everyone's uniqueness may bring conflict into the team if the team loses sight of the goal. An effective team builds on the wide range of skills contributed by the team members.

Mentors and mentees are a two-person team with membership in a larger team of the school or special education department. They share a connectedness, rather than an official team shirt. They share the same goals or norms. They make decisions with both members' input; the relationship builds on the gifts both bring to the team. And like teams with more than two members, mentors and mentees need time to form and plan before they begin work.

Engagement

Mentor pairs work best when a task or goal is set out before them. This is the same as Vella's concept of engagement. She writes of engaging learners in activities to help the adult learners who are engaged in the process of learning. By establishing an action plan for the mentor and mentee at the beginning of the year, activities are selected and progress can be measured.

Accountability

The final principle of adult learning is accountability. Along the way we have described several other principles that have accountability built into them. The sequencing and reinforcement, praxis, and clear roles principles all integrate some type of accountability in them. Why is this important to adult learners? Adult learners invest time and effort to improve their skills at a conscious level, unlike children who improve skills because they must. Adults want to see a pay off for their effort. Members of a mentoring pair have to commit to success and demonstrate success as an outcome.

Begin the mentoring relationship by finding out what mentees feel they need. Add to that list of needs the contextual constraints that will figure heavily into a successful first year of teaching. From this *needs assessment,* an action plan is built to focus the mentees' efforts during the year. The needs assessment helps build a respectful relationship between mentors and mentees. This *respect for the learner* assures adult learners that mentors are supporters, not evaluators. By the end of the first semester, a mentor-mentee pair should see themselves as a *team,* with shared goals, shared concerns, and shared support. If they can attend meetings together (both in and outside of their school), the bond becomes even stronger.

As the mentoring relationship builds, the degree of comfort the pair feels should also build. A sense of *safety* increases as the relationship deepens. As the mentee and mentor come to know more about each other, they find similarities and connections between themselves. By *clarifying the roles* of the members, the pair is better able to discuss and share. This strengthens the pairing.

The first year of teaching is, to say the least, overwhelming. To attempt to learn all the skills a teacher must possess would be enough to cause the strongest teachers to doubt their professional abilities. The mentor and mentee need to select and prioritize tasks to complete during the first weeks of school, before the first parent conference, before the first marking period ends, and so forth. By performing prioritizing tasks, they *sequence and reinforce* the learning that needs to occur during the first semester of school. By thoughtfully sequencing the tasks to be undertaken, the special education mentee finds accomplishments in small steps. The *immediacy* of reinforcement is the motivator for the new special education teacher, enabling the continued learning of new skills.

Over the course of the first months of school, the mentoring pair should take the opportunity to *reflect* on the accomplishments and challenges (see the activities timeline in Resource E). To reflect, the mentor may need to model the thinking process that goes on when one reflects on their actions. The pair may use video or audiotaping to help reflect on a teaching episode. When the mentoring pair talks about their practice, the mentor should make the reflections as comprehensive as possible, considering the *concepts, feelings, and actions* that go into the decision-making process used.

It is necessary to consider how rapidly new ideas, feelings, and actions are addressed and acted upon. If the pair undertakes too much too soon, then the mentee may not feel as if they have had time to master anything. If they execute a task too slowly, then the mentee may feel as if the mentor is held back. Pacing in mentoring, as in teaching, is very important. When a teacher attempts to just "cover" the curriculum, students may not learn the material. Just "covering" new skills with a new teacher will not fully *engage* the mentee in the learning process.

The last element of adult learning is accountability. Because the pairing is truly a team, there is *accountability* on both members' parts. That does not mean that the mentor is judged on the mentee's success. Rather, the pair should mutually rejoice in successes and sweat over the challenges.

ADULT LEARNING THEORY

How Adults Learn. Knowles (1990) based his andragogical model on several assumptions that describe how adults learn.

1. Adults need to know why they must learn something before they will set about learning it. Relevance is the key concept. Adult learners need to know that new knowledge is relevant to their job, their family, and their life. Mentors, therefore, are in the business of helping new special education teachers become aware of what they need to know.

2. Adult learners have an established self-concept that includes an understanding of their capability to make decisions for themselves. Granted, some very young adults are still learning how their decisions affect their lives, but they have an established track record of making decisions (both good and bad) that impact their own life. One interesting comment Knowles made about adults and self-concept stated:

   > Once they have arrived at that self-concept they develop a deep psychological need to be seen by others and treated by others as being capable of self-direction. They resent and resist situations in which they feel others are imposing their wills on them. (Knowles, 1990, p. 58)

Validating Experience. Knowles goes on to explain the reaction teachers have when they attend inservice and training sessions as an example of discounting the power of self-concept in governing adult learning. Teachers are notorious for attending inservice sessions and almost daring the presenter to "Try to teach me." *For mentors, the relationships they have to build with their mentees include reality-based feedback.* The special education mentor provides feedback that is grounded in real experiences and reaffirms the mentee's self-concept.

1. Adults arrive with real life experiences. For better or worse, the experiences we have had influence how we behave and the decisions we make. They even delineate how we describe ourselves. Even our student teaching experiences influence our perceptions. If we discount or reject the experiences another has had, we are in essence discounting or rejecting that individual. The mentor needs to provide feedback to the mentee about the quality of the decisions made. What better way to ensure that the mentee will continue to make quality decisions than to model the decision-making process with the mentee through descriptive feedback.

2. Adults are ready to learn. Just as children go through different developmental stages during which they are increasing their knowledge or increasing their physical stature, adults go through developmental stages in which they are increasing their knowledge. They are ready to learn. The hardest part of teaching adults is timing the support to coincide with the adult's readiness to learn. The mentor's task is to provide enticing new knowledge. What is enticing? Typically, the information they need to have is very motivating.

3. Adults are life-centered in their orientation to learning. Adults will expend energy on completing tasks or learning new skills to the extent that they see a pay off in their work life. These new skills are learned even more rapidly when they are presented in a personal context. For example, veteran special education teachers will commit themselves to after-school workshops and curriculum activities to learn the newly adopted reading curriculum because they see the real-life application to their own classroom.

4. The most powerful motivators for most adults are those related to job satisfaction, self-concept, and quality of life. Money and more responsibility factor into motivation, but Knowles posits that these external motivators usually are not as powerful as those that motivate internally. The continual growth in some adults is blocked in others when a lack of resources, time, or opportunity occurs. The job of the mentor is to help the mentee find resources or look for opportunities to keep motivation high.

Motivation. Adult-learning theory rests on the idea that adults are motivated to change and learn new concepts and skills when the new concepts are presented in a way that connects to their life. Teachers love to see how an innovation will help them *today*. Mentors must be mindful of the adult's desire to improve when it is clearly linked to their current needs. Mentors must keep in mind the many variables influencing the mentee's needs.

Mentors must consider the adult learner's preexisting self-concept. The sense of personal strength and weakness requires honest feedback that shapes the self-concept, rather than destroys it. Adults are motivated from within to excel. A special education mentor can build on this internal motivation by connecting the mentee's new ideas with a success-oriented outcome. The more success the mentee experiences, the more their motivation and self-concept increases.

STYLES OF LEARNING/ PERSONALITY TYPES

Because we cannot assume that adult learners come to a new situation with no preconceived ideas or skills, then we have to understand that the ways adults learn are habitual. Their personality is a function of reinforced patterns and satisfying outcomes. Some psychologists use the outcomes from personality measures, such as the Myers-Briggs Type Indicators (MBTI) as a way to describe patterns of behavior and communication. In the mentoring relationship, knowing the best way to communicate with your mentee helps the relationship grow stronger, faster.

The MBTI (Briggs-Myers & McCauley, 1962) as described by Thomas Denham (2002) is a self-reporting tool that allows adults to examine their own communication and personality styles to help with interpersonal relationships. In the workshop sessions for mentor training in Resource A, it is suggested that the mentor workshop trainer use the MBTI as a way to help mentors understand how they communicate. This will help mentors understand how they are coming across to their mentees and in turn facilitate the growth of the relationship.

WHAT IF?

You are the mentor of a very new and very energetic special education teacher. When you are discussing how you prepare your class for year-end testing, your mentee indicates that, "I would never do it that way." You of course do not want to discourage the new teacher, but you also know from experience how the special education students respond to the year-end testing. After you express your opinion and offer assistance, your mentee still thinks, "I'll do it my way." What do you do?

Possible Solutions

1. Assure the mentee that both plans will benefit the students but indicate that it may be a good idea to take data along the way to determine if the prep process she is using is more efficient. After all, if it works, shouldn't others know about it too?

2. Describe the process you use and offer specific tips on how to use that process in a classroom. Offer suggestions, but let the new teacher try his or her own ideas.

REFERENCES

Bloom, B. S. (1953). The thought process of students in discussion. In S. J. French (Ed.), *Accent on teaching: Experiments in general education* (pp. 23–46). New York: Harper & Brothers.

Briggs-Myers, I., & McCauley, M. H. (1962). *Introduction to type: A description of the theory and application of the Myers-Briggs Type Indicator* (10th ed.). Palo Alto, CA: Consulting Psychological Press.

Denham, T. (2002). *A technical review of the Myers-Briggs Type Indicator*. [EDRS document]. Retrieved June 8, 2003, from http://www.edrs.com/Webstore/Download.cfm?ID=721658

Fawcett, G. (1997). Is a good teacher always a good mentor? *Mentor Network Journal, #1*. Retrieved June 15, 2003, from http://www.mentors.net/Library.html

Knowles, M. (1984). *Andragogy in action: Applying modern principles of adult learning.* San Francisco: Jossey-Bass.

Knowles, M. S. (1990). *The adult learner: A neglected species* (4th ed.) Houston, TX: Gulf Publishing.

Vella, J. (2002). *Learning to listen, learning to teach: The power of dialogue in educating adults.* San Francisco: Jossey-Bass.

Resource A

Action Plans

Table A.1 ESE mentee-mentor action plan template

Mentee Name: _____   Mentor Name: _____

School: _____   School: _____

District: _____

Date Written:

Target Review Date: _____

Target Review Date: _____

Target Review Date: _____

Target Review Date: _____

Goals to Accomplish: 1. _____

2. _____

3. _____

4. _____

"What" (What you will do)	"So What" (How you will do it)	"Now What" (How will you reflect on the outcome)
Goal 1.	1.	1.
Goal 2.	2.	2.
Goal 3.	3.	3.
Goal 4.	4.	4.

EXAMPLE MENTEE-MENTOR ACTION PLANS

Table A.2   Example elementary ESE mentee-mentor action plan

Mentee Name: *Marta Higgins*   **Mentor Name:** *Wendy Case*
School: *Everglades Elementary*   **School:** *Everglades Elementary*
District: *Marlby*
Date Written: August 27, 2004
Target Review Date:* *September*   **Target Review Date:** *February*
Target Review Date: *October*   **Target Review Date:** *March*
Target Review Date: *November*   **Target Review Date:** *April*
Target Review Date: *January*   **Target Review Date:** *May*
* or more frequently as needed

Goals to Accomplish: 1. *Increase the number of specific praise statements used in each class period.*
2. *Increase positive classroom climate by decreasing students' verbal interruptions during instruction to one per lesson.*
3. *Improve long-range planning to develop four thematic units.*
4. *Complete courses required to maintain temporary ESE certification.*

"What" (What you will do)	"So What" (How you will do it)	"Now What" (How will you reflect on the outcome)
Goal 1. Increase my specific academic praise statements to a minimum of ten per hour.	1. Post a visual cue. 2. Set a timer for 10 minutes. 3. Audiotape myself and listen for specific academic praise.	1. If I meet the goal, then I'll remove the visual prompt. 2. I'll try this technique with my fourth period class as well as my first period class.
Goal 2. Decrease the number of Balt's verbal outbursts to no more than one per day.	1. Develop an intervention strategy with mentor. 2. Recognize Balt's frustration signs.	1. Try this technique with another student making verbal outbursts. 2. Conduct a functional assessment of behavior to identify antecedents and consequences of behavior.
Goal 3. Develop eighteen lesson plans for a semester-long thematic unit on Florida's Everglades.	1. Research needed information and gather planning forms prior to meeting with mentor. 2. Co-plan the unit with mentor.	1. Refine activity to use with next year's students. 2. Reflect on what went well and what could be improved in this unit.
Goal 4. Register for six credit hours at the local university to meet certification requirements.	1. Ask my mentor if she knows local universities. 2. Search university course schedules online for needed courses.	1. Evaluate my professional and personal goals. 2. Join a professional organization.

Table A.3   Example high school ESE mentee-mentor action plan

Mentee Name: *Bill Waddle*   **Mentor Name:** *Serena Johnson*
School: *Jupiter High*   **School:** *Jupiter High*
District: *Palm*
Date Written: August 13, 2004
Target Review Date:* *September*   **Target Review Date:** *February*
Target Review Date: *October*   **Target Review Date:** *March*
Target Review Date: *November*   **Target Review Date:** *April*
Target Review Date: *January*   **Target Review Date:** *May*
* or more frequently as needed

Goals to Accomplish: 1. *Participate in a classroom management workshop.*
2. *Observe teachers with effective classroom management skills.*
3. *Practice using reflective thinking after teaching a lesson.*

"What" (What you will do)	"So What" (How you will do it)	"Now What" (How will you reflect on the outcome)
Goal 1. Participate in a classroom management workshop.	1. Check school district inservice calendar. 2. Check local university's course schedule. 3. Register and participate in workshop.	1. Successful participation in either a workshop or course 2. I will discuss classroom management techniques presented in the workshop with my mentor and implement at least one new technique after the workshop.
Goal 2. Observe teachers with effective classroom management skills.	1. Observe a science teacher, recommended by my mentor, at my school.	1. Conference with my mentor and the science teacher after the observation to discuss effective techniques.
Goal 3. Practice using reflective thinking after teaching a lesson.	1. I will observe my mentor teaching and discuss her planning process using a guided think aloud. 2. Use the reflective thinking guide in Chapter 5 to reflect on pre-, interactive, and postplanning using a think aloud. I will do this after I teach a lesson for five consecutive days.	1. I will have a completed planning guide to use as a model. 2. I will complete the planning guide and meet with my mentor to discuss areas of strength and need.

Resource B

CEC Standards and Mentoring Resources

The Council for Exceptional Children (CEC) is considered the learned society for the field of special education. The significance of this label is that teacher preparation programs across the United States, and indeed internationally, look to the CEC for guidance on the goals and directions for the field. The CEC developed and validated the core knowledge and skills needed by special education teachers by describing the roles and responsibilities of today's special education professionals. The most recent version of the CEC Knowledge and Standards incorporated the 10 Interstate New Teacher Assessment and Support Consortium (INTASC) core principles into their most recent edition of the *CEC Code of Ethics and Standards for Professional Practice for Special Education* (5th ed.). This publication provides performance-based standards that can be adopted by teacher education programs to ensure quality graduates. For the purposes of this book we have excerpted the structure of the *Code of Ethics and Standards* to provide an overview of the resource. The book of ethics and standards is available in its entirety through the CEC Web site at http://www .cec.sped.org/ps/code.html.

CEC PROFESSIONAL TEACHING STANDARDS

There are ten teaching standards central to the CEC professional standards. The ten teaching standards are the minimum knowledge, skills, and dispositions inherent in a quality special education program. Each standard is broken down into observable outcome measures. The outcome measures include general disposition, knowledge, and skill sets as well as those germane to specialty areas such as gifted, vision impaired, hearing impaired, and early childhood. Skill sets are also available for teachers assigned to programs that are "individualized general" curriculums (corresponds to most mild and moderate or high-incidence disability categories) and for those in "individualized independence" programs (corresponds to most severe or profound certification).

Standard #1: Foundations

Special educators understand their field as an evolving and changing discipline based on philosophies, evidence-based principles and theories, relevant laws and policies, diverse and historical points of view, and human issues that have historically influenced the education and treatment of individuals with exceptional needs, both in school and in society. Special educators understand how these influence professional practice, including assessment, instructional planning, implementation, and program evaluation. Special educators understand how issues of human diversity can impact families, cultures, and schools, and how these complex human issues can interact with issues in the delivery of special education services. They understand the relationships between special education organizations and the organizations and functions of schools, school systems, and other agencies. Special educators use this knowledge as a ground upon which to construct their own personal understandings and philosophies of special education.

Standard #2: Development and Characteristics of Learners

Special educators know and demonstrate respect for their students first as unique human beings. Special educators understand the similarities and differences in human development and the characteristics between and among individuals with and without exceptional learning needs. Moreover, special educators understand how exceptional conditions can interact with the domains of human development, and they use this knowledge to respond to the varying abilities and behaviors of individuals with exceptional learning needs. Special educators understand how the experiences of individuals with exceptional learning needs can impact families, as well as the individuals' ability to learn, interact socially, and live as fulfilled, contributing members of the community.

Standard #3: Individual Learning Differences

Special educators understand the effects that an exceptional condition can have on an individual's learning in school and throughout life. Special educators understand that the beliefs, traditions, and values across and within cultures can affect relationships among students, their families, and the school community. Moreover, special educators are active and resourceful in seeking to understand how primary language, culture, and familial backgrounds interact with the individual's exceptional condition to impact the individual's academic and social abilities, attitudes, values, interests, and career options. The understanding of these learning differences and their possible interactions provides the foundation upon which special educators individualize instruction to provide meaningful and challenging learning for individuals with exceptional learning needs.

Standard #4: Instructional Strategies

Special educators possess a repertoire of evidence-based instructional strategies to individualize instruction for individuals with exceptional learning needs. Special educators select, adapt, and use these instructional strategies to promote positive learning results in general and special curricula and to appropriately modify learning environments for individuals with exceptional learning needs. They enhance the learning of critical thinking, problem solving, and performance skills of individuals with exceptional learning needs, and increase their self-awareness, self-management, self-control, self-reliance, and self-esteem. Moreover, special educators emphasize the development, maintenance, and generalization of knowledge and skills across environments, settings, and the life span.

Standard #5: Learning Environments and Social Interactions

Special educators actively create learning environments for individuals with exceptional learning needs that foster cultural understanding, safety and emotional well-being, positive social interactions, and active engagement of individuals with exceptional learning needs. In addition, special educators foster environments in which diversity is valued and individuals are taught to live harmoniously and productively in a culturally diverse world. Special educators shape environments to encourage the independence, self-motivation, self-direction, personal empowerment, and self-advocacy of individuals with exceptional learning needs. Special educators help their general education colleagues integrate individuals with exceptional learning needs in general education environments and engage them in meaningful learning activities and interactions. Special educators use direct motivational and instructional interventions for individuals with exceptional learning needs to teach them to respond effectively to current expectations. When necessary, special educators can safely intervene with individuals with exceptional learning needs in crisis. Special educators coordinate all these efforts and provide guidance and direction to paraeducators and others, such as classroom volunteers and tutors.

Standard #6: Language

Special educators understand typical and atypical language development and the ways in which exceptional conditions can interact with an individual's experience with and use of language. Special educators use individualized strategies to enhance language development and teach communication skills to individuals with exceptional learning needs. Special educators are familiar with augmentative, alternative, and assistive technologies to support and enhance communication of individuals with exceptional needs. Special educators match their communication methods to an individual's language proficiency and cultural and linguistic differences. Special educators provide effective language models, and they use communication strategies and resources to facilitate understanding of subject matter for individuals with exceptional learning needs whose primary language is not English.

Standard #7: Instructional Planning

Individualized decision making and instruction is at the center of special education practice. Special educators develop long-range individualized instructional plans anchored both in general and in special curricula. In addition, special educators systematically translate these individualized plans into carefully selected shorter-range goals and objectives, taking into consideration an individual's abilities and needs, the learning environment, and a myriad of cultural and linguistic factors. Individualized instructional plans emphasize explicit modeling and efficient guided practice to assure acquisition and fluency through maintenance and generalization. Understanding these factors, as well as understanding the implications of an individual's exceptional condition, guides the special educator's selection, adaptation, and creation of materials, and the use of powerful instructional variables. Instructional plans are modified based on ongoing analysis of the individual's learning progress. Moreover, special educators facilitate this instructional planning in a collaborative context including the individuals with exceptionalities, families, professional colleagues, and personnel from other agencies as appropriate. Special educators also develop a variety of individualized transition plans, such as transitions from preschool to elementary school and from secondary settings to a variety of postsecondary work and learning contexts. Special educators are comfortable using appropriate technologies to support instructional planning and individualized instruction.

Standard #8: Assessment

Assessment is integral to the decision making and teaching of special educators, and special educators use multiple types of assessment information for a variety of educational decisions. Special educators use the results of assessments to help identify exceptional learning needs and to develop and implement individualized instructional programs, as well as to adjust instruction in response to the ongoing learning progress. Special educators understand the legal policies and ethical principles of measurement and assessment related to referral, eligibility, program planning, instruction, and placement for individuals with exceptional learning needs, including those from culturally and linguistically diverse backgrounds. Special educators understand measurement theory and practices for addressing issues of validity, reliability, norms, bias, and interpretation of assessment results. In addition, special educators understand the appropriate use and limitations of various types of assessments. Special educators collaborate with families and other colleagues to assure nonbiased, meaningful assessments and decision making. Special educators conduct formal and informal assessments of behavior, learning, achievement, and environments to design learning experiences that support the growth and development of individuals with exceptional learning needs. Special educators use assessment information to identify supports and adaptations required for individuals with exceptional learning needs to access the general curriculum and to participate in school system and statewide assessment programs. Special educators regularly monitor the progress of individuals with exceptional learning needs in general and special curricula. Special educators use appropriate technologies to support their assessments.

Standard #9: Professional and Ethical Practice

Special educators are guided by the profession's ethical and professional practice standards. Special educators practice in multiple roles and complex

situations across wide age and developmental ranges. Their practice requires ongoing attention to legal matters along with serious professional and ethical considerations. Special educators engage in professional activities and participate in learning communities that benefit individuals with exceptional learning needs, their families, colleagues, and their own professional growth. Special educators view themselves as lifelong learners and regularly reflect on and adjust their practice. Special educators are aware of how their own and others' attitudes, behaviors, and ways of communicating can influence their practice. Special educators understand that culture and language can interact with exceptionalities, and they are sensitive to the many aspects of diversity of individuals with exceptional learning needs and their families. Special educators actively plan and engage in activities that foster their professional growth and keep them current with evidence-based best practices. Special educators know their own limits of practice and practice within them.

Standard #10: Collaboration

Special educators routinely and effectively collaborate with families, other educators, related service providers, and personnel from community agencies in culturally responsive ways. This collaboration assures that the needs of exceptional learners are addressed throughout schooling. Moreover, special educators embrace their special role as advocates for individuals with exceptional learning needs. Special educators promote and advocate the learning and well-being of individuals with exceptional learning needs across a wide range of settings and a range of different learning experiences. Special educators are viewed as specialists by a myriad of people who actively seek their collaboration to effectively include and teach individuals with exceptional learning needs. Special educators are a resource to their colleagues in understanding the laws and policies relevant to individuals with exceptional learning needs. Special educators use collaboration to facilitate the successful transitions of individuals with exceptional learning needs across settings and services.

The No Child Left Behind Act (NCLB) (2001) discusses support for all levels of teachers to ensure quality teachers. Although the legislation recommends career ladders and professional development, it leaves the door open to the states to develop other support programs that provide professional development and to increase retention rates. Many state boards of education have included mentoring programs as a way to retain and support teachers. Below is a chart from the Education Commission of the States (1999) containing the most recent practices in mentoring prior to NCLB from across the country. Sixteen states mandate *and* fund induction programs for all new teachers. These induction programs typically include mentoring programs. In addition, teachers who attain National Board Certification are required to mentor new teachers as part of maintaining their National Board Certification.

STATE SUPPORT FOR NEW TEACHERS

Table B.1   State support for new teachers

	INDUCTION/MENTORING/SUPPORT						
	State has an induction program for new teachers	**State requires *and* finances induction for all new teachers**	**Duration of mentoring required by state (years)**	**Amount of time state requires mentors and their assigned teachers to meet**	**State requires mentors and teachers to be matched by school, subject, and/or grade level**	**State requires release time for mentors**	**State requires mentors to be compensated for their work**
ALABAMA							
ALASKA							
ARIZONA							
ARKANSAS	√	√	1	1 HOUR PER WEEK	√	√	√
CALIFORNIA	√	√	2		√		
COLORADO	√		1				
CONNECTICUT	√	√	1	1 MEETING PER WEEK		√	√
DELAWARE	√	√	3				√
DISTRICT OF COLUMBIA	√		1	1 MEETING PER WEEK			√
FLORIDA							
GEORGIA							
HAWAII							
IDAHO	√	√	1				
ILLINOIS							
INDIANA	√	√	1		√		√
IOWA	√	√	2			√	√
KANSAS							
KENTUCKY	√	√	1	70 HOURS PER YEAR	√	√	√
LOUISIANA	√	√	2				
MAINE	√		2	6 MEETINGS PER YEAR			
MARYLAND	√		1	40 MINUTES PER WEEK			
MASSACHUSETTS	√	√	1			√	
MICHIGAN	√		3		√		
MINNESOTA	√						
MISSISSIPPI	√		1	90 HOURS PER YEAR			

(Continued)

Table B.1 (Continued)

	INDUCTION/MENTORING/SUPPORT						
	State has an induction program for new teachers	State requires and finances induction for all new teachers	Duration of mentoring required by state (years)	Amount of time state requires mentors and their assigned teachers to meet	State requires mentors and teachers to be matched by school, subject, and/or grade level	State requires release time for mentors	State requires mentors to be compensated for their work
MISSOURI	√		1				
MONTANA							
NEBRASKA							
NEVADA							
NEW HAMPSHIRE							
NEW JERSEY							
NEW MEXICO	√	√	1				
NEW YORK							
NORTH CAROLINA	√	√	3				√
NORTH DAKOTA							
OHIO	√	2004	1				
OKLAHOMA	√	√	1	72 HOURS PER YEAR	√		
OREGON							
PENNSYLVANIA	√		1				
RHODE ISLAND							
SOUTH CAROLINA	√	√	1				
SOUTH DAKOTA							
TENNESSEE							
TEXAS	√		1				
UTAH	√						
VERMONT	√		2				
VIRGINIA	√	√	1		√		
WASHINGTON	√					√	√
WEST VIRGINIA	√	√	1	1 HOUR PER WEEK	√	√	
WISCONSIN	√						
WYOMING							
U.S.	31	16	—	—	8	7	9

NOTE: From Education Commission of the States. (1999). *Beginning teacher mentoring programs.* Retrieved on April 13, 2004, from http://www.ecs.org/clearinghouse/13/15/1315.doc. Adapted with permission.

REFERENCES

Council for Exceptional Children. (2003). *What every special educator must know: The international standards for the preparation and certification of special education teachers* (5th ed.). Arlington, VA: Author.

Education Commission of the States. (1999). *Beginning teacher mentoring programs.* Retrieved on April 13, 2004, from http://www.ecs.org/clearinghouse/13/15/1315.doc

National Board for Professional Teaching Standards. (n.d.). *Renewal Standards.* Retrieved on January 6, 2004, from http://www.nbpts.org/standards/index.cfm

U.S. Department of Education (2001). *No Child Left Behind Act of 2001.* Washington, DC. Retrieved on July 29, 2004, from http://www.ed.gov/nclb/landing.jhtml

Resource C

Professional Resources

This resource section contains reference information for special education journals, professional organizations, video and textbook resources, and assessments. Ordering information is provided, and, when available, a Web site that provides more information is included with the entry.

JOURNALS

Communication Disorders Quarterly

Pro-Ed, Inc.
8700 Shoal Creek Boulevard   Austin, TX 78757
Telephone: (800) 897–3202   Fax: (800) 397–7633
Web site: http://www.proedinc.com/
Publishing schedule: Four times per year

Exceptional Children

Council for Exceptional Children
1110 North Glebe Road, Suite 300   Arlington, VA 22201–5704
Telephone: (703) 620–3660   Toll-free: (888) CEC–SPED
Fax: (703) 264–9494
Web site: http://www.cec.sped.org
Publishing schedule: Four times per year

Focus on Exceptional Children

Love Publishing Company
9101 East Kenyon Avenue, Suite 2200   Denver, CO 80237
Telephone: (303) 221–7333   Fax: (303) 221–7444
Web site: http://www.lovepublishing.com/
Publishing schedule: Nine times per year

FOCUS on Learning Problems in Mathematics

Center for Teaching/Learning of Mathematics
PO Box 3149   Framingham, MA 01701
Telephone: (781) 235–7200
Web site: http://www.unlv.edu/RCML/index.html
Publishing schedule: Four times per year

Intervention in School and Clinic

Pro-Ed, Inc.
8700 Shoal Creek Boulevard   Austin, TX 78757
Telephone: (800) 897–3202   Fax: (800) 397–7633
Web site: http://www.proedinc.com/
Publishing schedule: Five times per year

The Journal for Vocational Special Needs Education

National Association of Vocational Education Special Needs Personnel
Web site: http://www.cew.wisc.edu/jvsne/
Publishing schedule: Three times per year

Journal of Learning Disabilities

Pro-Ed, Inc.
8700 Shoal Creek Boulevard   Austin, TX 78757
Telephone: (800) 897–3202   Fax: (800) 397–7633
Web site: http://www.proedinc.com/
Publishing schedule: Six times per year

Learning Disability Quarterly

Council for Learning Disabilities
PO Box 4014   Leesburg, VA 20177
Telephone: (571) 258–1010   Fax: (571) 258–1011
Web site: http://www.cldinternational.org/
Publishing schedule: Four times per year

Math Notebook

Center for Teaching/Learning of Mathematics
PO Box 3149   Framingham, MA 01701
Telephone: (781) 235–7200
Web site: http://www.unlv.edu/RCML/index.html
Publishing schedule: Monthly newsletter

Preventing School Failure

Heldref Publications
1319 Eighteenth Street Northwest   Washington, DC 20036
Telephone: (202) 296–6267
Fax: (508) 296–5149
Web site: http://www.heldref.org
Publishing schedule: Four times per year

Remedial and Special Education

Pro-Ed, Inc.
8700 Shoal Creek Boulevard   Austin, TX 78757
Telephone: (800) 897–3202   Fax: (800) 397–7633
Web site: http://www.proedinc.com/
Publishing schedule: Six times per year

Research and Practice for Persons With Severe Disabilities

Association for Person With Severe Handicaps
29 West Susquehanna Avenue, Suite 210   Baltimore, MD 21204
Telephone: (410) 828–8274   Fax: (410) 828–6706
Web site: http://www.tash.org/
Publishing schedule: Four times per year

Teaching Exceptional Children

Council for Exceptional Children
1110 North Glebe Road, Suite 300   Arlington, VA 22201–5704
Telephone: (703) 620–3660   Fax: (888) CEC–SPED
Web site: http://www.cec.sped.org
Publishing schedule: Six times per year

PROFESSIONAL ORGANIZATIONS

American Association on Mental Retardation

444 North Capitol Street Northwest, Suite 846
Washington, DC 20001–1512
Telephone: (202) 387–1968   Toll-free: (800) 424–3688
Fax: (202) 387–2193
Web site: http://www.aamr.org

Council for Exceptional Children (CEC)

1110 North Glebe Road, Suite 300 Arlington, VA 22201–5704
Telephone: (703) 620–3660
Web site: http://www.cec.sped.org
CEC has the following specialty divisions teachers can join:
Council of Administrators of Special Education (CASE)
Council for Children with Behavioral Disorders (CCBD)
Division for Research (CEC-DR)
CEC Pioneers Division (CEC-PD)
Council for Educational Diagnostic Services (CEDS)
Division for Communicative Disabilities and Deafness (DCDD)
Division on Career Development and Transition (DCDT)
Division on Developmental Disabilities (DDD)
Division for Culturally and Linguistically Diverse Exceptional
    Learners (DDEL)
Division for Early Childhood (DEC)
Division of International Special Education and Services (DISES)
Division for Learning Disabilities (DLD)
Division for Physical and Health Disabilities (DPHD)

Division on Visual Impairments (DVI)
The Association for the Gifted (TAG)
Technology and Media Division (TAM)
Teacher Education Division (TED)

Council for Learning Disabilities

PO Box 4014   Leesburg, VA 20177
Telephone: (571) 258–1010   Fax: (571) 258–1011
Web site: http://www.cldinternational.org

The International Dyslexia Association

Chester Building, Suite 382
8600 LaSalle Road Baltimore, MD 21286–2044
Telephone: (410) 296–0232   Fax: (410) 321–5069
Web site: http://www.interdys.org

National Alliance of Black
School Educators (NABSE)

310 Pennsylvania Avenue Southeast   Washington, DC 20003
Telephone: (202) 608–6310   Fax: (202) 608–6319
Web site: http://www.nabse.org/

National Center for Learning Disabilities

381 Park Avenue South, Suite 1401   New York, NY 10016
Telephone: (212) 545–7510   Toll-free: (888) 575–7373
Fax: (212) 545–9665
Web site: http://www.ld.org

VIDEOS

Classroom Management

How Difficult Can This Be? The F.A.T. City Workshop

PBS Videos (1974)
Web site: http://www.shoppbs.org

Learning Disabilities and Discipline: When the Chips Are Down

PBS Videos (1997)
Web site: http://www.shoppbs.org

Winning at Teaching . . . Without Beating Your Kids

Kids Are Worth It! (1990)
Web site: http://www.kidsareworthit.com

IEPs and Self-Determination

Self-Directed IEP

Sopris West (1996)
Web site: http://www.sopriswest.com

Whose Decision Is It Anyway?

Program Development Associates (1997)
Web site: http://www.disabilitytraining.com

Inclusion

Regular Lives

PBS Videos (1996)
Web site: http://teacher.shop.pbs.org

TEXT RESOURCES: CLASSROOM MANAGEMENT

Canter, L., & Canter, M. (1992). *Lee Canter's assertive discipline: Positive behavior management for today's classroom.* Santa Monica, CA: Lee Canter & Associates.
  ISBN: 0–939007–45–2
  Web site: http://www.canter.net
  Toll-free: (800) 262–4347

Jones, F. H. (2000). *Tools for teaching.* Santa Cruz, CA: Fredric H. Jones & Associates.
  ISBN: 0-9650263–0-2
  Web site: http://www.fredjones.com
  Telephone: (831) 425–8222

Sprick, R., Garrison, M., & Howard, L. (1998). *CHAMPs: A proactive and positive approach to classroom management for grades K–9.* Longmont, CO: Sopris West.
  ISBN: 1–57035–166-X
  Web site: http://www.sopriswest.com
  Telephone: (303) 651–2829   Toll-free: (800) 547–6747

TEXT RESOURCES: FIRST YEAR OF TEACHING

Cohen, M. K., Gale, M., & Meyer, J. M. (1994). *Survival Guide for the First-Year Special Education Teacher* (Rev. ed.). Reston, VA: Council for Exceptional Children Publications.

ISBN: 0–86586–256–7
Web site: http://www.cec.sped.org
Toll-free: (888) CEC-SPED

Wong, H. K., & Wong, R. T. (1988). *The first days of school: How to be an effective teacher.* Mountain View, CA: Harry K. Wong Publications.
ISBN: 0–96293602–2
Web site: http://www.effectiveteaching.com
Telephone: (650) 965–7896

ASSESSMENT RESOURCES

Pierangelo, R., & Giuliani, G. (1998). *Special educator's complete guide to 109 diagnostic tests.* West Nyack, NY: Center for Applied Research in Education.

A useful and comprehensive compendium for tests for special education can be found in Pierangelo & Giuliani's (1998) book entitled *Special Educator's Complete Guide to 109 Diagnostic Tests.* This resource describes the most frequently used assessments. The text can serve as a reference to check age appropriateness, validity and reliability information, and availability for the tests included.

New special education teachers learn to use assessments in the trenches. Their preservice course work probably has prepared them to give some tests that are widely used, but district-specific tests may be foreign to them. They are often the recipients of tests and test scores completed by other professionals. New special educators need to interpret test data much more frequently than they need to collect formal test data. A supportive mentor should talk about when and why a specific test is given and how to decide which test to use for a specific assessment need. For example, special education teachers may be required to assess student reading skills at the year's end. Which test should they select for comprehension? Which for decoding? Does it matter? Can we use teacher-made tests? A mentor can guide the mentee through the decision making process by using a think aloud procedure to help the mentee understand why and how to select a specific test.

Resource D

Mentor Workshop

This mentor workshop can be offered in a two-day format or broken up over time. There are advantages to both formats. By having the training session for the mentors condensed into a two-day period, the critical information that is needed by the mentors is delivered early in the mentoring process. The mentors meet their mentees after they have all the foundational information. The advantage to providing ongoing support to mentors over the course of an entire semester or year is that the mentors not only get the needed information, but they also are able to meet periodically and discuss issues related to mentoring in their school or district. Program designers should consider the intended outcomes of the mentoring program and select the staff development model that best suits their goals and needs.

Workshop Goals

1. To identify needs of beginning special education teachers.

2. To learn interpersonal communication skills needed to mentor.

3. To demonstrate, via role-playing, effective problem-solving techniques.

4. To identify four ways mentors can help new special education teachers transition to teaching.

5. To help the mentee clarify yearly goals by using an action plan.

6. To evaluate the program's success.

Workshop Anticipated Outcomes

1. Increase the numbers of new special education teachers who remain in the school and district.

2. Support veteran special education teachers by recognizing quality teaching through mentoring.

3. Socialize new special education teachers to their schools and strengthen their connection to their schools.

Materials

Name tags

Markers

Poster-size paper for group notes

Welcome and Introductions

Begin by saying, "Congratulations and thanks for being here. Mentoring takes time and commitment on the mentor's part."

Review the plan for the day's or days' activities.

Thinking Back to Being a New Teacher

To be an effective mentor, you have to remember what it was like to be a new teacher. Start off the morning's activities by breaking the group into four smaller groups, and have them share an experience with their group that sticks in their mind about their first year of teaching. After about 30 minutes of small-group chatter, pull the groups back together and ask them to come up with a "completer" for the following prompt. Have the groups write their responses on a poster-sized sheet of paper.

Prompt: One thing I wish I knew then that I know now about the first year of teaching is . . .

Lead the discussion to include the following ideas:

- You have to celebrate the small victories

- You can't save all the kids this year, but you can save one

- This job can't be done by yourself

- Everyone develops survival skills

- Everyone thinks they are just faking at teaching

Teaching: The First Year

Ellen Moir (1999) wrote about keeping in mind everything that new teachers go through to make the mentoring process more effective. Review what Moir described as the phases of a teacher's first year.

The first phase is *Anticipation Phase*. This phase begins during student teaching, just as the assignments are finishing up, and the student can actually see herself as a teacher next year. This excitement revolves around making a commitment to making a difference. It includes romanticizing the role of the teacher. Idealism and excitement characterize the first few weeks of the school year.

By October the new teacher has entered the second phase—the *Survival Phase.* During this phase the new teacher is overwhelmed with learning a million new things, some very *big* (like curriculum and management) and some very small (like bus duty and taking attendance). No matter how small, they all take on gargantuan proportions. One of the biggest concerns is developing curriculum. Veteran teachers have old lesson and unit plans from which to draw when developing teaching materials. The new teacher, however, is constantly making new things for every lesson. The new teacher is moving forward at a breakneck pace.

The third phase of a teacher's first year is the *Disillusionment Phase.* After about eight weeks of high-intensity stress, the new teacher is plagued by thoughts of incompetence. He or she starts making comments like "It should-n't be this hard. Maybe I'm not cut out for teaching." This is underscored by having to conduct parent conferences and not knowing how to describe plans for the rest of the year. New special education teachers typically have difficulty planning for the rest of the week! Added to this is the toll the stress takes on the teacher's physical health. The only ray of hope during this phase is that winter break is near.

The fourth phase is the *Rejuvenation Phase.* After break, beginning in January, the teacher comes back with an improved attitude. Like spring weather, the change is slow, but a positive attitude eventually makes an appearance. The rejuvenation phase is not a smooth one, some ups and downs still occur. When year-end testing arrives, the teacher again questions herself about her ability to be the best teacher for her students.

The final phase is the *Reflection Phase,* and it begins during the last six weeks of school. The teacher begins to reflect on the year—not the small problems, rather the whole picture. She begins to make plans for the next year, especially in the areas of management, curriculum, and teaching strategies. This reflection phase allows the new special education teacher to return to the anticipation phase with which he or she began the year.

Mentors will find it helpful to keep in mind the phases and needs within each phase when working with new teachers. As a veteran, you can tell they need help with management, but they may not be ready to hear that or ready to work on that skill. They have other things that seem more pressing, such as the policies and procedures for the school or developing lesson plans. The successful mentor gives the mentee what he or she needs in the time frame they can handle it.

Making the Communication Connection

After talking about how it was when we started teaching and what new teachers need when they start teaching, we need to begin building skills related to mentoring new teachers. The first skill to develop is effective communication techniques. The way people communicate is based on their personalities, their likes and dislikes, and their style of problem solving. By understanding how we communicate, we can better understand how to communicate with others. This process is very much like identifying learning styles or preferences. One vehicle for identifying your personality type is the Myers-Briggs questionnaire.

There are two online locations for the Myers-Briggs. The first one is a long, seventy-question survey of attitudes. The second one is a four-question belief sorter. If we were going to do this to match mentors with mentees, then the seventy-question survey would be more accurate. However, we are doing this just to talk about styles and preferences. Therefore, the four-question sorter works for the purposes of this training.

For the seventy-question version go to http://www.advisorteam.com/user/ktsintr01.asp

For the four-question version go to http://www.haleonline.com/psych/

After completing the Myers-Briggs, talk about what the letters mean

One resource is the Web document "Working out your Myers-Briggs type." This document is available online at http://www.teamtechnology.co.uk/tt/t-articl/mb-simpl.htm

Table D.1   Possible symbols for the Create a Mentor activity

Big Heart	Cares for members of the community, including students and their families, faculty, and staff
Ready Smile	Has a kind smile for all
Big Ears	Listens actively, and reflects the best ideas back to the mentee
Juggling Balls	Designs, implements, and evaluates instruction for her own students while helping with mentee needs
On a Pedestal	Seen by others (teachers and administrators) as an effective teacher, good manager, and all-around excellent role model
Flip-Top Head	Is open-minded to suggestions and new ideas from others
Magnifying Glass	Helps clarify problems—makes the options seem clearer
Bag of Tricks	Has the ability to put her hands on many resources
Cheerleader	Always there on the sidelines, cheering others on

When finished describing the characteristics of each type, bring the discussion around to talking about communication style. Ask the mentors to consider what makes them comfortable or uncomfortable in communicating with others? Their mentees may or may not have the same style as they do. Therefore communication styles may or will vary. Reading nonverbal signs and listening to them is crucial to make the mentoring relationship work.

Communication is the key to a positive mentoring relationship. We start communicating effectively when we have the same ideas or goals in mind. Let's start by getting the same definitions and descriptions. Have the group develop a picture of what a mentor and a mentee are. To do this, break the group again into subgroups of four members each. Give each group a poster-sized sheet, some markers, and the Symbols sheet (see Table D.1). (Optional materials could include glitter, colored paper, cloth, buttons, etc.)

The Ideal Mentor

Directions: Each group uses the provided materials to create the ideal mentor by incorporating the symbols into their pictures.

Table D.1 shows some possible symbols for the Create a Mentor activity. (Groups can develop others that they need for the activity.)

After about 30 minutes, have each group display and describe their "perfect mentor." Finish the discussion by making comments about the role of the mentor being "a guide on the side—not a sage on the stage." To be that guide, some practice with communication skills may be needed. The next activities are intended to help mentors practice communication skills.

CONFERENCING SKILLS

Carl Glickman (2002) has a handy book on leadership skills that help teachers succeed. Early in his book *Leadership for Learning: How to Help Teachers Succeed,* Glickman places the behaviors and techniques used by instructional leaders on a continuum that represents communication skills from nondirective through collaborative to directive. These skills are exactly what mentors need in their repertoire for working with new teachers. Glickman's behavior continuum follows. He uses the instructional leader (principal) as the key for each role, but for our purposes we have substituted mentor for instructional leader.

Maximum Teacher Responsibility

Listening: The mentor sits quietly, looks at the speaker, and nods her head to show understanding. Nodding and furthering responses (e.g., "ummmm," etc.) also indicate listening.

Clarifying: The mentor asks questions and restates to clarify the speaker's point of view: "Do you mean . . . ?," or "Would you explain this further?"

Encouraging: The mentor provides acknowledgment responses that help the speaker continue to explain his or her positions: "OK, I think I understand. Tell me more. . . ."

Reflecting: The mentor summarizes and paraphrases the speaker's message for verification of accuracy: "So the issue is. . . ."

Presenting: The mentor gives his or her own ideas about the issue being discussed: "This is how I see it. . . ."

Problem Solving: The mentor takes the initiative, usually after a preliminary discussion of the issue or problem solutions, in pressing all those involved to generate a list of possible solutions. This is usually done through statements such as "Let's stop and each write down what can be done," "What ideas do you have to solve the problem?"

Negotiating: The mentor moves the discussion from possible to probable solutions by discussing the consequences of each proposed action, exploring conflicts or priorities, and narrowing down choices with questions such as "Can we find a solution that will suit all the parties?"

Directing: The mentor tells the mentee either what the choices are or what should be done. The mentor may need to explain the choices and the follow-up process by saying, "We need to proceed in this way. . . ."

Standardizing: The leader sets the expected criteria and timeline or time frame for the decision to be implemented: "By next Monday we should see. . . ."

Reinforcing: The mentor strengthens the directive and criteria to be met by describing the possible consequences. Possible consequences can be stated in a positive way by summarizing with the statement in the form of praise: "I know you can do it!" Consequences can also be negative: "If it's not done, we will lose the support of. . . ."

Maximum Leader Responsibility

The mentor will most often use the more collaborative behaviors on the continuum (i.e., listening through problem solving). Occasionally they will need to get down to directive behaviors to help a mentee figure out a plan. Be cautious! Being directive can disable a mentee. When mentors tell the mentee how to solve a problem or negotiate an outcome, they are effectively absolving the mentee from developing a solution of his or her own. Mentees are more likely to develop a solution by themselves if they are given a chance and a little support (not direction) from their mentors. It's the same as the idea in the Chinese proverb: "Give a man a fish and you feed him for a day. Teach a man to fish and you feed him for a lifetime" (Tripp, 1970, p. 76). The following skills are the ones most frequently used by mentors in continuing their relationships with their mentees.

Reflective Listening. Listening is a crucial skill for mentors. It is not an easy task to be a good listener because many things interfere with a person's ability to listen effectively. Rehearsing a response, daydreaming, stumbling over controversial words or ideas, filtering messages, and being distracted by the details are just a few. If a listener is constantly jumping for a chance to talk or respond, he or she may miss the intent of the message or the hidden message in the conversation. Likewise avoiding or fixating on hot topics or controversial words may mask the real message. Of all the distractions, the one that can cause the most problem is message filtering. This refers to the listener's ability to turn off the message because he or she either does not have a frame of reference for the conversation or has an overfamiliarity with the topic. For example, the speaker wants to talk about a topic that has already been covered extensively at a recent faculty meeting. You don't want to hear about it anymore—or talk about it anymore, so you tune out. That's filtering. Or you are talking with someone who is sharing information that you know nothing about—you tune out because you can't make the connection to what they are sharing. That's filtering. This is a troublesome distraction because, if the speakers perceive that you have tuned out, they also perceive that what they have to say doesn't have value for you. In a mentoring relationship, this does more harm than expected.

Activity to Practice Effective Listening. Divide into groups of three. One member of the group is a speaker, one is a listener, and one is an observer. The speaker speaks to the listener for three minutes. The listener listens but does not give any feedback, verbal or nonverbal. The observer watches the pair during the monologue, attending to body language and individual behavior.

Stop the groups at three minutes and ask for comments. How hard was this activity? What did you notice? Was this communication? Why?

Do the activity again, switching roles within the groups. This time have the speaker speak for three minutes, but the listener is allowed to give nonverbal feedback. Stop the groups at three minutes, and ask for comments. How hard was this? What did you notice? Was this communication? Why?

Cognitive Coaching

Cognitive coaching attends to the thought processes used during planning, teaching, and reflecting phases. It is typically observed when mentees express their feelings about problems they are having. Usually they want the mentor to solve the problems for them. The role of the mentor is not necessarily to solve the problems, rather to help the mentee figure out a solution. Cognitive coaching is designed to be conducted between peers. It may be used by those in a hierarchical relationship, as long as the relationship includes mutual trust. However, cognitive coaching should not be used for evaluation purposes. Within the mentoring situation, the cognitive coaching model puts the mentee in charge of the coaching process, with the goal being change in teacher thinking, leading to a change in behavior or teaching pedagogy. The coach nonjudgmentally listens to the observations made by the mentee and asks questions that make the mentee reflect on his or her thinking.

The power is in the questioning techniques, because the questions cause the mentee to reflect and think about his or her teaching and modify it for the future. The questioning techniques of cognitive coaching include open-ended questions, paraphrasing what the mentee said, and clarifying and probing questions to delve more deeply into the thinking of the new teacher. The questions are used as part of the conferencing, which precedes teaching and occurs after teaching.

Self-Analysis of Communication Skills. Again, have the mentors break into groups and devise a way to analyze their communication skills. Have the groups consider how they will know if they are effectively employing communication skills. Possibilities include the development of checklists or scenarios to help them evaluate their own skills. They should include the following skills (and any others they wish to add):

- Listens without interrupting

- Accepts mentee's point of view

- Identifies important points

- Summarizes, paraphrases, and clarifies

- Interprets nonverbal language to self and possibly to mentee

- Pursues issues assertively

- Reinforces mentee's efforts

Bring the groups back together, and discuss how they chose to evaluate their own styles. Were there any commonalities, or did any new and interesting ideas arise?

Problem Solving

Working with another teacher places the mentor in a curious position. You should not be put in the position of evaluating the mentee, but you will certainly be asked by others how the new teacher is doing. Your relationship with your mentee is one built on trust and support. New teachers trust their mentors to help them with the "big stuff." Sometimes the big stuff is what administrators feel all teachers should know how to do: Either know it or leave. Your job as a mentor is to help the mentee figure out how to do this job we call teaching. Your problem-solving skills are crucial to mentoring. The following scenarios are included to help mentors practice their communication and problem-solving skills.

Problem-Solving Scenarios

Have the mentors work either with each other or as a large group to discuss solutions for each scenario. Both communication and problem-solving skills will be practiced.

Scenario #1 Your mentee is an out-of-field special education teacher. He comes from a sales background and does not have an education degree or experience in education. The needs assessment he has completed indicates that he needs help in understanding the paperwork, completing IEPs, keeping documentation, and understanding the psychological report. He has indicated that he has everything in the classroom under control, but he believes his students are unmotivated and stupid.

Scenario #2 Your mentee calls you at home in tears. She has made a big mistake. Although she has spent the last four years completing her degree in education, she now realizes that she is "not cut out" for teaching. The demands of her job are too great. She is bringing home hours of work every evening and has no time for her life. She is totally stressed out and feels ready to break.

Scenario #3 Your mentee is having problems with his administrator. He feels that he is being targeted and treated unfairly. He knows that he is having difficulty with behavior management, but much of this is due to having a class of twenty students in his high school cross-categorical special education class that meets in a classroom designed as a resource room.

Scenario #4 Your mentee is not cooperating with you. You have tried to establish a relationship with him, however, you receive extreme resistance. He is older than you and from a culture that is very different from yours. He has his doctorate in psychology. You have heard from other sources that he doesn't think he needs a mentor, especially a woman!

Scenario #5 You meet with your mentee. Although you feel he needs assistance in his classroom, he continues to bring the conversation back to his personal life. This is a second career for him. He left a lucrative business due to downsizing and thought that teaching would be a fulfilling opportunity.

He is having difficulty making ends meet on a beginning teacher's salary. He has a big mortgage and a family to support. His wife refuses to work, insisting on staying home to homeschool their five children.

Scenario #6 You have been working with your mentee for several months. He has identified some areas of concern, and you two have developed a plan of action to meet his needs. His principal has called you into his office to confide that he is thinking of letting him go. He wants your input.

Scenario #7 Your mentee is the worst teacher you have ever seen and has no clue how bad he is. He has no regard for the students, using humiliation as a means of behavior control. He doesn't seem prepared for lessons and has large periods when he has nothing prepared at all except a video that is not related to the curriculum. The class is out of control, and it is painful for you to be there.

Scenario #8 Your mentee is a very promising new teacher. She has spirit and drive. She cares for the students and seems to have a lot of great teaching skills. Her department chair has asked her to do things with which she doesn't feel comfortable. He has brought her IEPs to sign, when she hasn't been in attendance. He assures her that they do it like this all the time because they cannot get teachers released from their classes to attend meetings. She finds one student with an IEP that lapsed at the end of last year. He says there is no problem, they will just write a new one and backdate it. After all, the parent never shows anyway.

FOUR WAYS MENTORS CAN SUPPORT NEW TEACHERS

In Susan Villani's book, *Mentoring Programs for New Teachers* (2002), she discusses four things mentors can do to support new teachers. These points are summarized in the following paragraphs:

- **Provide emotional support and encouragement.** New teachers leave teaching for many reasons: some because they are underprepared, some because they were not aware of the realities of the world of teaching, others because they were not recruited specifically for their teaching abilities. In each of these cases, the necessary support and encouragement varies. Using the information about your own styles and skills, underscored in this training, will help you lend the emotional support a mentee needs. Your goal is to reinforce the worth and good intentions of each new special education teacher; that's encouragement and support of the highest quality!

- **Provide information about the daily workings of the school and the cultural norms of the school community.** We talk about helping special education students understand the hidden curriculum to get by in school. We need to do the exact same thing with mentees. Tell them the little-known facts that might be helpful. The smallest tip is worth it. Where are the best parking spots? Can you wear jeans? Should they go to the pep rally? Helping

them understand the hidden curriculum or the cultural norms helps them fit in and save face a "million" times a day.

- **Promote cultural proficiency regarding students and their families.** This relates to the school and community culture and the one from which the new teacher comes. The mentor can help the mentee understand what the community expects from a teacher. Again these tips allow the mentee to work more effectively and to avoid embarrassing situations.

- **Cognitive coaching.** We've already talked about cognitive coaching as a part of the mentor's skill repertoire. Villani also talks about how an effective cognitive coaching model in the induction year can lead to a very effective peer-coaching model for continued improvement over the teacher's career.

Supports From Mentors

Mentors provide differing levels of support to their mentees. The first level of support to consider is *low*-intensity supports. This type of support answers the following questions: to whom to go, where to go, when should I do this, and what is this. The mentee wants to know the basics. They are in "need to know" mode. This information is crucial to running a class and just keeping their heads above water. The second level of supports are *high*-intensity supports. Typically, high-intensity supports require the mentor and mentee to interact much more closely and intensely than just talking or sharing. High-intensity supports require modeling and think-alouds, observing and becoming an emotional sounding board. A mentor should look at ways to help the mentee with low-intensity supports before jumping to the high-intensity supports. The idea is that the lower-intensity supports allow the mentees to develop their own style of teaching rather than just doing what someone else does without thinking about why they are doing it. It's the "fish for a lifetime" idea again.

Villani describes the process of beginning a mentoring relationship as similar to orienting someone to a new place. She uses the analogy of visiting Yellowstone National Park for the first time to study the reintroduction of wolves to the wild. First, you would want to know your way around the park and know who the other rangers are by name if possible. Then you would want to ask specific questions about where you could get the supplies you need for your work. You would also want to know about any rules the park has about how to work in the park and if all the rules are written down, or some are implied. The park ranger who is showing you around would probably want to know more about the project, but since you are in the beginning stages of the project, the information you might have would be sketchy. So the park ranger has to draw the information out and get at the center of your plan.

What Do Mentors Do?

In this activity the mentors identify what type or intensity of support they might need to give to a mentee in the situations listed below. This list comes from Kathleen Feeney Jonson's book, *Being an Effective Mentor: How to Help Beginning Teachers Succeed* (2002). Put the list on the overhead and have the groups of mentors decide what level of intensity would be needed in each instance. Some will be able to go either way (low or high); ask what might prompt a low-intensity response versus a high-intensity response.

Classroom management

Lesson planning

Time management (how to get things done)

Communicating with parents, other teachers, and so forth

Administrative tasks (IEPs, open house, grade books, etc.)

Being a Mentor

The mentoring process begins by getting to know each other and learning what each person's role is in the relationship. The mentor needs to build trust with the mentee and the mentee needs to see the mentor as a resource, not a repair person. By taking the tour around Yellowstone, the mentee can get a sense of what the role of the mentor is, but this role needs constant reinforcing so that the mentee doesn't cast the mentor into a conflicting role. The action plan described later will help with the role-clarification aspect of the relationship.

To build trust, the mentor must demonstrate openness, honesty, and candor. A sharing person is less likely to inflict harm. Certainly, it goes without saying that the sharing and candor should be professional and appropriate for the situation. The best way to develop trust is to listen with concern and empathy. We are likely as mentors to jump in and solve the problems new teachers present. However, just listening to and encouraging the mentee is more effective than supplying the answers (Jonson, 2002, p. 109).

The next step is to develop a plan. This mentoring training includes a mentor-mentee action plan as a way to accomplish the following:

- Clarify the roles and responsibilities of the mentor and mentee

- Provide a focus and framework for mentor-mentee teamwork

- Become an informative resource when shared with others

The concept of action planning is very similar to IEP planning, so special education teachers should not have great difficulty in understanding how to use and develop these plans. The plans we are using come from Jonson's book on *Being an Effective Mentor* (pp. 144–147). The goals identified should be short-term, that is, they should be attainable within a few months. Plans should be reevaluated two or three times a year so the beginning teacher can gain a sense of attainment. Crossing off goals that were met is a powerful motivator and almost as good as stickers and stars! Keep in the back of your mind that the new teacher has more than a few staff development sessions to attend. This is particularly true of those who are not only new to teaching but also those teaching out-of-field. They will certainly have difficulty juggling all the required components of a new teacher program, and they may see mentoring as an added time waster if the action plan is not developed with consideration of the overall work demands.

Action Planning

The sample action plan included in this training packet is for elementary special education pairs. It may be helpful to break the mentors into pairs at similar grade levels and have them role-play mentor and mentee as they complete an action-planning form (see Tables D.2 and D.3).

Table D.2   Action plan form

Mentor-Mentee Action Plan

Mentee: _____

Mentor: _____

Date: _____

Four Priority Goals for the Year

i.

ii.

iii.

iv.

Objectives	Activity (what, who, where, dates)	Evidence of Completion/Successes

Table D.3   Sample action plan

Sample Mentor-Mentee Action Plan

Date: _____

Mentee: _____

Mentor: _____

Four Priority Goals for the Year

  i. To obtain a broad view of teaching styles and strategies

 ii. To develop mastery of resource room curriculum

iii. To maximize time spent on learning tasks

iv. To develop on-the-job collaboration skills

Objectives	Activity (what, who, where, dates)	Evidence of Completion/Successes
1. Broaden view of styles and strategies Become familiar with three new teaching strategies. Attempt to use one new strategy.	Do observation in multiage classrooms (Nov.). Take coursework in curriculum integration (10 clock hours Jan. and Feb.). Have debriefing sessions following observations. Attend behavior supports workshop (Jan. 25).	Observed at Starlight Elem. on Nov. 9: • Guided reading group strategy • Integrated daily living skills into curriculum • Viewed instructional tapes on positive behavior supports
2. Mastery of curriculum Build bank of instructional strategies. Become familiar with teaching resources.	Locate videotapes, and books that support units of study. Obtain a list of extended-level reading materials.	• Knows who to contact for resources at district and within school. • Implemented alternative strategy that resulted in greater time on task in resource room • Had observations and debriefing focusing on teaching and student responses
3. Time on task Improve time management. Increase time on task within classroom.	Have observer collect data relevant to time on task in Oct. and Nov. Brainstorm different mgmt. strategies. Increase awareness of teaching styles through reflection, observation, feedback, and analysis.	• New strategy resulted in increase in time on task • Observations and debriefings focused on teaching techniques • Increased independent learning time • Positive class environment; less time spent on discipline
4. Developing collaborative skills Work with mentor to develop home-school communication. Develop connection with general staff.	Work on newsletter for parents. Select one faculty member to work with on math curriculum.	• Showcase newsletters • Worked with Ms. Peterson on third-grade math units

FADING SUPPORT

One of the hardest things to identify in a mentor-mentee relationship is when to let go. The mentor has invested so much in the relationship; not just time, but emotional support, concern, and professional skills have been shared between the pair. The mentor has to observe objectively to know when the mentee is ready to take a leadership role in the relationship.

The mentor has to determine when to allow the mentee is ready to take "flight," sometimes identified as supportive release. In Herbert Kindler's book on *Managing Disagreement Constructively* (1988, p. 38), he describes supportive release as a conscious decision to support and encourage a person's initiative. The mentor may or may not agree with a mentee's decision, or plan of action, but will decide to unconditionally support the individual's efforts. Of course this would never occur if the mentor believed that harm or inappropriate outcomes would result from the mentee's action.

The typical process for fading support is to fade one type of support at a time, or to change the type of support to a less-intensive style. In other words, the mentor will move from professional support to social support or lessen the amount of time spent on professional support.

ONGOING SUPPORT

All the possible preparation is of little value if we haven't addressed the mentor's concerns. Close the session with a discussion using open-ended statements. Be sure to listen to the mentors' comments and fears. These statements will help us provide support to the mentors as they are working with their mentees.

What Happens If?

Have the mentors read and respond to the following open-ended statements. These can be done individually, but the mentors should be given a little time to think about their responses to the statements before sharing them with the group.

What happens if . . .

- My mentee leaves

- The match doesn't work

- I don't like this mentoring thing

- This is the best thing ever

TRAINING EVALUATION

To evaluate the training content and effectiveness, we plan on evaluating the participants' opinions at the end of the trainings and then again at the end of the school year. The session leader should hand out the evaluation form and have the participants respond on the sheet. Indicate that the responses will be kept confidential.

POST-TRAINING EVALUATION

At the first meeting with my mentee . . .

Based on my personality, my biggest mentoring challenge will be . . .

The best thing about mentoring for me will be . . .

The most useful thing I learned from this training is . . .

The ways I "exude" approachability are . . .

I plan to deal with my frustrations as a mentor by . . .

REFERENCES

Glickman, C. D. (2002). *Leadership for learning: How to help teachers succeed.* Alexandria, VA: ASCD.

Jonson, K. F. (2002). *Being an effective mentor: How to help beginning teachers succeed.* Thousand Oaks, CA: Corwin Press.

Kindler, H. S. (1988). *Managing disagreement constructively: Conflict management in organizations.* Los Altos, CA: Crisp Publications.

Moir, E. (1999). The stages of a teacher's first year. In M. Scherer (Ed.), *A better beginning: Supporting and mentoring new teachers.* Alexandria, VA: ASCD.

Tripp, R. T. (Ed.). (1970). *The International Thesaurus of Quotations.* New York: Perennial Library.

Villani, S. (2002). *Mentoring programs for new teachers: Models of induction and support* (pp. 9–13). Thousand Oaks, CA: Corwin Press.

Resource E

Timeline for Mentoring Activities

Table E.1   Timeline for mentoring activities

Mentor–Mentee Activities Timeline		
Month	**Activity**	**Accomplishment**
August—(Month 1)	Call or e-mail mentee prior to the start of school.	☐
	Make face-to-face contact with one another.	☐
	Share backgrounds and personal interests.	☐
	Give mentee a school tour.	☐
	Introduce mentee to faculty and staff.	☐
	Provide the mentee with a list of district forms and when to use them.	☐
	Give mentee completed copies of the most important district forms.	☐
	Complete the mentee needs survey.	☐
	Complete the mentor-mentee action plan.	☐
	Contact mentee daily during the first week of school.	☐
	Other:	☐
	Other:	☐
September—(Month 2)	Meet at least semimonthly to discuss issues such as the following:	☐
	• Classwide and individual discipline	☐
	• Efficient paperwork	☐
	• Managing time	☐
	• Planning for diverse student levels	☐
	• Writing IEPs	☐
	• The school culture	☐
	• School operating procedures	☐
	• Child study team procedures	☐
	Arrange to teach a demonstration lesson for the mentee.	☐

Month	Activity	Accomplishment
	Mentor–Mentee Activities Timeline	
	Follow up the demonstration with a debriefing.	☐
	Maintain ongoing communication as needed by phone, e-mail, or another method.	☐
	Review mentor-mentee action plan.	☐
	Other:	☐
	Other:	☐
October—(Month 3)	Meet at least semimonthly to discuss issues such as the following:	☐
	• Working with paraprofessionals	☐
	• Working with general education teachers	☐
	• Student discipline	☐
	• Long-term versus short-term lesson planning	☐
	• Grading student work	☐
	• Report cards	☐
	• Locating materials and resources	☐
	• Open house	☐
	• ESE week	☐
	• Professional organizations	☐
	Review the mentor-mentee action plan.	☐
	Meet for an activity out of school such as for a cup of coffee.	☐
	Brief the school principal about your mentor-mentee planning, not performance.	☐
	Other:	☐
	Other:	☐
November— (Month 4)	Meet at least semimonthly to discuss issues such as the following:	☐
	• The mentor-mentee action plan	☐
	• Curriculum materials	☐

Mentor–Mentee Activities Timeline		
Month	**Activity**	**Accomplishment**
	• Classroom transition time	☐
	• Planning field trips	☐
	• Mainstreaming/Inclusion	☐
	• Individual student discipline: Functional Behavioral Assessment	☐
	• Planning an instructional unit	☐
	Schedule for the mentee to observe the mentor's (or another teacher's) teaching in their own classroom. Focus on one particular area to observe.	☐
	Debrief the mentee's observation thoughts.	☐
	Attend a professional development workshop or seminar together.	☐
	Other:	☐
	Other:	☐
December–(Month 5)	Meet at least semimonthly to discuss issues such as the following:	☐
	• Communicating with parents	☐
	• Data collection	☐
	• Stress management	☐
	• School procedures regarding holiday activities	☐
	• Assistive technology	☐
	• Preparing students for the holiday break	☐
	Brief the school principal about your mentor-mentee planning, not performance.	☐
	Other:	☐
	Other:	☐
January–(Month 6)	Review the mentor-mentee action plan and set new goals if needed.	☐
	Meet at least semimonthly to discuss issues such as the following:	☐

Mentor–Mentee Activities Timeline		
Month	**Activity**	**Accomplishment**
	• Becoming a reflective thinker	☐
	• Effective learning strategies	☐
	• Dealing with isolation	☐
	• Curricular planning	☐
	• Increasing parent involvement	☐
	• Student discipline	☐
	Reassure the mentee that he or she is doing a good job, and identify specific examples.	☐
	Celebrate successes.	☐
	Other:	☐
	Other:	☐
February–(Month 7)	Meet at least monthly to discuss issues such as the following:	☐
	• Understanding a psychological report	☐
	• 504 plans versus IEPs	☐
	• Changing a student's placement	☐
	• Testing accommodations	☐
	• Preparing students for state-mandated testing	☐
	• Vocational evaluations	☐
	Meet again outside of school for coffee.	☐
	Review the mentor-mentee action plan.	☐
	Schedule an observation of the mentee's teaching.	☐
	Debrief the observation.	☐
	Brief the school principal about your mentor-mentee planning, not performance.	☐
	Other:	☐
	Other:	☐

Mentor–Mentee Activities Timeline		
Month	**Activity**	**Accomplishment**
March—(Month 8)	Meet at least monthly to discuss issues such as the following:	☐
	• Writing measurable annual goals	☐
	• Using norm-referenced assessments	☐
	• Community-based instruction	☐
	• Writing a transition IEP	☐
	• Teacher certification	☐
	• Sponsoring a school club	☐
	Arrange for the mentee to observe another teacher teaching.	☐
	Other:	☐
	Other:	☐
April—(Month 9)	Meet at least monthly to discuss issues such as the following:	☐
	• Supplemental aids and services	☐
	• Transitions (such as elementary school to middle school, middle school to high school, and school to work)	☐
	• Fading mentor support	☐
	• Action research in the classroom	☐
	• Evaluating student performance	☐
	Review the mentor-mentee action plan.	☐
	Brief the school principal about your mentor-mentee planning.	☐
	Other:	☐
	Other:	☐
May—(Month 10)	Meet at least monthly to discuss issues such as the following:	☐
	• End-of-school-year procedures	☐
	• Student paperwork to complete	☐
	• Documentation of the mentor-mentee activities	☐
	• Organization of materials over the summer	☐

Mentor–Mentee Activities Timeline		
Month	**Activity**	**Accomplishment**
	Plan for the beginning of the next academic year.	☐
	Evaluate the district's mentoring program, and offer suggestions for improvement.	☐
	Other:	☐
	Other:	☐

Index